GW00707703

6/24   £3

Fateful Beauty

BY

Natalie Hodgson

To Tim ~ Andrea
With love
Natalie Hodgson
06. 08. 06

Published by Eye Books

Fateful Beauty
1st Edition
2006

Published by Eye Books Ltd
8 Peacock Yard
London
SE17 3LH
Tel: +44 (0) 8454508870
website: www.eye-books.com

Set in Latinskij and Edwardian Script
ISBN:9781903070505

British Library Cataloguing in Publication Data
A catalogue record for this book is available from the British Library

Printed and bound in Great Britain by CPD Ltd

Acknowledgment

I would like to thank my nephew Graham Davidson for his encouragement. As secretary of the Coleridge society, he gave me confidence that the story had a value and a place and I hope that having read it you will agree.

My thanks also go Bill and Micky Hiscocks who have helped in so many ways in getting this book published.

I hadn't heard of Frances Coke until I came across Natalie Hodgson's biography which recounts her murky history in a very readable fashion. Without the encumbrance of footnotes of academic pretension, reading groups looking for good non-fiction will find much to debate herein. It only remains to note that at the age of 93, Natalie has added yet another string to her accomplished bow.

Guy Pringle editor Newbooks Magazine

I have always been passionate about books, and as someone who has had the privilege of meeting Natalie Hodgson, I wish her every success with this book, which is well researched and involves an issue that is close to the author's heart, independence of the individual.

Anna Druett owner of The Guardian Bookshop of the Year - Wenlock Books

My interest in this book is not only that part of it takes place in my Shropshire constituency and that Natalie Hodgson is one of my constituents, but more significantly because Sir Edward Coke, father of the heroine Frances Coke, introduced The Petition of Right to Parliament in 1628. This contribution to parliamentary democracy was, and still remains, fundamental. The characters in this story of love, intrigue, betrayal and tragedy have been carefully researched and set in the historical context of a significant time in the development of democracy in our land. A worthwhile read, not only for the Shropshire interest, but also for all those who enjoy history; and all who enjoy a good story

Phillip Dunne. M.P. & Co-Founder of Ottakar's

Foreward

Although I was not born in Shropshire I am proud to think of myself as "Shropshirebred", having spend much of my childhood there, my father being the Rector of Astley Abbotts and Linley, and, during the war, of Willey. Our family home was the Rectory at Astley Abbotts.

I am honoured to have been asked to write a foreward to this book by Natalie Hodgson, on the life of Frances Coke (1602-1642). Not only is there the link of Shropshire but both the author and the heroine are remarkable women.

Natalie's life has involved her in a great many things, including the Political Warfare Executive during the last war and later, while bringing up a family, she was elected to the County Council, worked with the Regional Health Authority, became a glider piolot, and travelled widely (to name but a few of her interests and achievements!) Sadly widowed in 1989, after 51 years of marriage, she still lives in Astley Abbotts where she has a 4 acre lavender farm which she lovingly looks after, as well as having bees, from which she makes and sells honey. At 93, she remains a popular, engaging, attractive and much admired member of the community, and retains an interest and vitality in all aspects of life and a concern for fairness and human rights, with a special interest in women's rights.

Francis Coke was the daughter of Sir Edward Coke who was the Lord Chief Justice, and although he believed passionately in freedom of the individual, he regarded women as chattels, with the result that to further his political career, he forced his daughter to marry John Villiers, the mentally handicapped brother of the King's favourite George Villiers.

Natalie Hodgson cares deeply about women who are trapped by events outside their control and she tells the enthralling story of the short and dramatic life of Francis Coke who died in poverty in Oxford, at the age of 40.

Sir Peter Gadsden. GBE, AC, FREng.

Lord Mayor of London. 1979-80

This is for my three children,
Robin, Duncan and Idonea.

CONTENTS

Bleeding Heart Yard

Y ou can still visit Bleeding Heart Yard, close to the
ceaseless traffic of Holborn Viaduct. You can tread
on the cobbled paths and see the lofty archway that once led
into bustling stables, but this and nearby Hatton Gardens
are all that remain to remind us that on this site once stood
a great Elizabethan mansion – Hatton House.

In its imposing hall on 11th November in the year 1588,
Edward Coke stood, awaiting his bride with an air of quiet
satisfaction. It was growing dusk as he looked out of the
window, the blue smoke from a myriad chimneys softening
and obscuring his view of Whitehall where all his hopes
were centred.

An ambitious man, he reviewed his life with some
satisfaction – from grammar school boy in Norwich to his
present position as Attorney General and Speaker of the

House of Commons. He had come far, but now he sought even greater heights and he looked to his new bride to help him. His first wife Bridget had borne him ten children, but brought him only a modest dowry. When she had died in June, just four months earlier, he had wasted little time in mourning, but hastened to find a suitable successor, a wife with money and, even more importantly, someone who could further his ambitions by having good court connections.

Now aged forty-six, he felt himself to be in his prime; his wit and wisdom were universally acknowledged, even feared, but he also realized that his swift advancement had made him many enemies, one of whom had written of him, 'his jewel of a mind was put into a fair case – a beautiful body with comely countenance, a case which he did wipe and keep clean, delighted in good clothes well worn, but a caustic tongue, disagreeable manners and an abominable temper.'

His bride-to-be, the Lady Elizabeth Hatton, kept him waiting awhile. It was on her insistence that the ceremony was to take place privately, in her own home in the evening. This was illegal and carried with it the threat of excommunication, but so determined was Edward Coke to secure the lady that he abandoned all his legal scruples and was prepared to give way to her every behest, reminding himself that he would have legal rights over her person and her fortune once their union was safely joined. He was only too aware that there were many other eager suitors, not least his great political rival, Francis Bacon, so he had pursued his courtship ardently, determined that no obstacle would hinder their marriage.

At last Elizabeth entered the hall, and he gazed at her admiringly as she walked slowly towards him, leaning on her father's arm. She was indeed beautiful – a young widow, barely twenty years old. The snowy folds and pleats of her ruff outlined the delicate oval of her face; her jewelled bodice, sparkling in the reflection of the sconces, surmounted a wide farthingale which emphasized her slender waist. But for her bridegroom, her beauty was by no means her greatest charm.

She held the far bigger attraction of great wealth and high birth, for she had been born a Cecil, the foremost family at court and one in high favour with Queen Elizabeth. With his intellect and her monies, which would shortly be his to enjoy, and the patronage which her family connections would bestow, he marvelled at his good fortune. Other people marvelled also and a contemporary wrote: 'Many were surprised that after so many large and likely offers, Lady Hatton should decline to a man of his qualitie and they will not believe that it was without some misterie.'

The old scandalmonger Aubrie believed he had solved the puzzle when he recounted that when the couple came to

3

bed, the bridegroom laid his hand on her belly and he felt a child stir. 'What,' quoth he, 'flesh in the pot?' to which she replied, 'Yes, or else I would never have married a cook.'

According to custom, parents arranged marriages for their children, partly to ensure their well-being, but often to enhance the family fortune, and love came after marriage, if at all. Her family had undoubtedly arranged her first marriage at the usual age of fourteen to Sir William Newport, a widower with one daughter only a few years younger than his new wife, and despite the age difference it was a most happy union. Sir William was a kindly man and proud of his beautiful young wife, whilst Elizabeth became firm friends with her little step-daughter.

Soon after the wedding Sir William inherited a great fortune from his uncle, Sir Christopher Hatton, but to claim it he was required to take the name of Hatton. This he readily did and the little family settled down in great happiness. Sadly only a few months after the death of his uncle and entering into his inheritance, Sir William was taken ill and all too soon followed Sir Christopher to the grave, leaving two desolate and grieving young women. At least they had no financial worries.

Whatever the reason Lady Hatton came to marry Edward Coke, whether it was family pressure or whether she had urgent personal reasons for a quiet and hasty wedding, she quickly came to regret it and often contrasted her subsequent misery with the short but happy time with her first husband.

The candles were burning low by the time the ceremony was over, and Edward Coke almost certainly murmured a silent prayer of thankfulness and relief as they completed their marriage vows and were pronounced man and wife. Now he had wealth previously undreamed of and connections to justify all his claims to promotion. His judicial and parliamentary duties required his frequent presence in London, where he could live in comfort in Hatton House, but that was by no means all his marriage brought him. His wife had inherited Corfe Castle with extensive lands around Purbeck, and she also had a substantial mortgage on a beautiful country estate at Stoke Poges, only twenty miles, or a day's coach journey, from London. He swiftly called in the mortgage and made Stoke Poges theirs.

He was quick to profit in other ways from his wife's estate, and Lady Hatton had her first unhappy premonition of the evil to come when her husband decided to sell the wardship of her stepdaughter for £4,000. She had promised Sir William that she would care faithfully for the child herself. Anyone buying a wardship could help themselves to the child's funds during infancy and then arrange a marriage to benefit themselves. Wardships were bought and sold, being highly lucrative and much sought after, and families anxiously tried to avoid them. For example, about this time Richard Sackville married in unseemly haste, without banns, a bride he hardly knew, because his father, the Earl of Dorset, was on his deathbed. Richard was only nineteen, so if unwed, he would have become a ward of the King who would have had the right to give or sell his wardship, but once safely married he no longer faced this danger.

Despite desperate protests, Edward Coke was adamant and his stepdaughter's wardship was sold, but that was only the start as he also refused to honour some legacies in Sir William's will. Aghast at his meanness and avarice, his wife refused to take the name of Coke until the legacies were paid and indeed she remained Lady Elizabeth Hatton for the rest of her life.

It was an inauspicious start, but Coke pursued his career relentlessly, and in 1601 they had the great honour and the monstrous expense of entertaining the Queen in their home at Stoke Poges where they duly presented her with the customary gifts to the value of a thousand pounds or more. What a commotion the visit caused, with the royal officials taking over the house a fortnight in advance to find suitable accommodation for the great officers of state, who never left the royal person, and for the ladies-in-waiting and the gentlewomen of the bedchamber. To Coke's great chagrin, the Queen did not knight him. For that he had to wait for the reign of King James who knighted almost anyone, particularly if they were willing to pay for it.

The couple settled down, none too amicably, sometimes together but often apart, either at Stoke Poges or at Hatton House. Their first child in 1599 was a daughter, Elizabeth, and there were some vague rumours of cuckoldry, and in 1602 they had a second daughter, Frances, this time indisputably his.

Unfortunately the joy of her birth was overshadowed by national mourning, for in March 1603 the great Queen Elizabeth died. She had been declining for a long time, and although her courtiers never dared to mention the matter of an heir, the Council of State, and indeed the whole country, was jittery. They dreaded a disputed succession and feared that the Catholics might advance the claim of Arabella Stuart with a possible invasion from the Continent to support her.

It was generally agreed that the crown was not likely to fall to the ground for want of heads to wear it, so a few hours after her death at Richmond, Robert Cecil, Secretary of State, acted swiftly. Summoning the Council of State to Whitehall at 10 o'clock, they pronounced James the new King. Cecil sent Sir Charles Percy and Thomas Somerset galloping north to Scotland to give James the welcome news and to enquire whether he would travel south by land or by sea. No one knew whether there would be any violent opposition, so ships were put to sea to repel any invaders and the country held its breath, and there was an eruption of joy when the succession passed without incident.

James had been waiting the summons with impatience, and decided to leave immediately, choosing to travel on horseback to meet some of his subjects on the way. Even the weather was kind and he rode south in a most beautiful English spring.

The new monarch made a good impression. He was thirty-seven years old, above average in height and an excellent horseman, he was witty and familiar with everyone, homely and coarse and apt to speak his mind only too freely. He delighted the populace when he shouted at a preacher who vexed him, 'I care not a turd for your preaching.' He looked his best on horseback because when walking his legs were spindly and his gait erratic. He had thinning brown hair, watery blue eyes and a tongue that was too big for his mouth which made him drink and speak 'very uncomely'.

The court went to meet him at York, where he had to pause and send to the Privy Council for funds, the first of many such requests. Everyone was anxious to make their mark with the new King and receive one of the many favours that he distributed liberally during the journey. Coke was among this number and he was duly knighted.

The Countess of Bedford was sent to escort the consort, Queen Anne of Denmark, and the royal children, and they travelled more slowly by coach. Lady Hatton waited on the Queen, and before long she became a close friend and was constantly in attendance at the court. The new Queen was frighteningly, deliciously extravagant; she liked jewellery and fine clothes and entertainment of every sort, and the court, which had been dull, uneventful and very parsimonious during Elizabeth's declining years, became amazingly alive and alarmingly bawdy, with a never-ending round of plays and masques, balls and river pageants.

Meanwhile Elizabeth and Frances remained at Stoke Poges with ponies and dogs, and governesses, tutors and servants to see to their every need. They were safer there, for 1603 brought a terrible outbreak of plague in which not less than 30,000 people died out of a population of some four million. In those years, plague and smallpox were a constant threat; infant deaths and mortality in childbirth occurred in every family and the average life expectancy was only thirty-six.

Since death often came so early, childhood too was short. Elizabeth and Frances learnt their lessons and also how to dance and sing. Their dancing tutor was paid 20 shillings a month. They learnt to ride, and at the age of four Frances had an old piebald pony and was able to accompany her sister who was already quite an accomplished rider. When she was five she was fitted with her first whalebone corset which was not very comfortable, but it made her feel grown-up as Elizabeth already wore one, and she accepted that she could no longer run and tumble in the grass as before.

Even more important was their education in the practicalities of running a large household, for Lady Hatton expected her daughters to marry the highest in the land. From earliest days they visited the cow byre and watched the dairymaids churning the butter in the dairy; they learnt to sew fine linen and embroider tapestry; they watched and joined in the preparation of jams and sweetmeats, of quince and damson cheese; they were taught how to salt meat for winter, for in those days a bad harvest meant real starvation and every large household had not only to support itself, but be prepared to help out the poor and the landless. They learnt the use of herbs to flavour dishes and to concoct simple medical remedies, and in late summer they picked and dried lavender to sweeten linen.

From time to time the great family coach would roll up and they would run to meet their parents, greeting them with curtsies and great respect. Lady Hatton would call them to her room to see her beautiful jewellery and dazzling court gowns. She would tell them stories of the goings-on at Whitehall, of one courtier who had his horses' hooves shod in silver and wore suits so covered with precious stones that no material was visible. She recounted stories of parties and pageants and admitted that sometimes they grew so rowdy and drunken that tables were overturned, clothes were torn and precious gold chains and jewels were lost or stolen.

Frances, in particular, was entranced by her mother's tales and longed to grow up, to enter this wonderland where she would be presented to the King and Queen about whom she had heard so much. The children played for hours, practising deep curtsies and elaborate bows as if they were at court.

While Lady Hatton served the Queen and the children grew up at Stoke Poges, Sir Edward's career became more erratic and much less peaceful.

King or Coke

Sir Edward Coke was proud, ambitious and confident, certain now that his talents would be recognized and rewarded. His secret aim was to become Chancellor, the highest administrative post in the Kingdom, and with his marriage, his wife's money and her excellent family connections, he felt that he could surely achieve that. However it was his misfortune to be at the epicentre of three titanic struggles, which would finally erupt in the great civil war of 1640, namely the tussle for supremacy between King and Parliament, the rift between the law courts and the ecclesiastical courts, and finally the simmering distrust between Protestants and Catholics.

From 1603, the year of James' accession, until 1617, Sir Edward fought ceaselessly, often too courageously for his own good, to defend the rights and privileges of Parliament, to assure the absolute supremacy of law and justice over both King and Parliament, whilst he resolutely opposed Catholicism and did his best to ensure that the laws against it were enforced.

Despite the jubilation at his accession, King James quickly estranged his subjects. He was naturally authoritarian, with a fervent belief in the divine right of kings and an even greater conviction of his own wisdom. Very early in his reign he forfeited the affection of the Puritans when he refused their plea for religious tolerance. Remembering only too vividly the humiliation he had suffered from Scottish ministers and his mother's cruel treatment by John Knox, he forbade the purpose of the dissenters. 'If you aim at a Scottish presbytery,' he stormed, 'it agreeth as well with a monarchy as God with the devil. I will make your party conform or harry them out of the land.' Nonconformity, he assured them, was not only heresy but also treason, since the King was head of the church.

Having antagonized a fair number of his subjects, he called the Lords and Commons to assemble in the great Hall of Westminster, where he lectured them saying, 'Consider the attributes of God, see how they agree in the person of a King: God hath power to create or destroy, to give life or send death, to judge all and be judged by none. So Kings make and unmake their subjects.' And on another occasion he informed Parliament that, 'the state of monarchy is the supremest thing on earth. To dispute with God is blasphemy; to dispute what a King may do is sedition. I will not be content that my power may be disputed upon.'

Most people accepted that monarchy was the natural form of government and agreed, albeit uneasily, that royal authority stemmed from God, but as a member of the House of Commons and particularly as its Speaker, Sir Edward was quite prepared to dispute the absolute royal prerogative in order to uphold the rights and privileges of Parliament. This was not always easy because Parliament only sat when it was summoned by the King, and if it displeased him, it was immediately prorogued. James disliked Parliament because it threatened his absolute power, but even he had to recognize that it was his sole source of legal funds, so he only summoned it when he urgently needed money and found himself unable to raise sufficient funds by various illegal means.

He sold titles, made laws by proclamation, and retrospectively fined those who offended; he sold monopolies to his courtiers – thus the Earl of Northampton had a monopoly on the sale of starch, very lucrative when starched ruffs were de rigueur, and the Earl of Nottingham had the monopoly on wine – but James' most hated habit of all was raising money by forced loans which were termed 'benevolencies'.

Sir Edward protested bravely against all these matters, declaring that they should be decided in Parliament; and greatly daring, he once declared that the King was *sub Deo et sub lege*, which so enraged James that Coke was forced to kneel and grovel at the royal feet.

His struggle against the church authorities also found him confronting the King. When England split from Rome, the Court of High Commission was set up to settle ecclesiastical disputes. Gradually it enlarged its power, assumed the right to fine and imprison and tried cases that should by rights have come to the law courts, and when the judges intervened and issued a prohibition on these cases, disputes were frequent and bitter. James very much liked having the two authorities so that he, the wise and just monarch, could arbitrate between them. He sided in most cases with the authoritarian Church and its much-feared Court of High Commission.

Sir Edward prospered and his prestige rose, both inside and outside Parliament, although not within his marriage where he still refused to honour Sir William Hatton's will. As Attorney General it was his duty to prosecute for the Crown and he went to his task with enthusiasm. An attack on Sir Walter Raleigh was unbelievably and unnecessarily vitriolic when he addressed him in court: 'Thou hast a Spanish heart and thyself art a spider of hell. I will now make it appear that there never lived a viler viper upon the face of the earth than thou.' As Raleigh was popular with the nation, this vituperation brought Sir Edward no friends but it inspired fear in his victims and condemned Sir Walter to fourteen long years in the Tower, and finally execution.

He was on far more popular ground when in 1605 he prosecuted equally ferociously at the trial of the Gunpowder Plot conspirators. He had no qualms about interrogating prisoners on the rack, indifferent to their sufferings – indeed he attended torture sessions to see that the proper degree of pain was inflicted and he was merciless to Guy Fawkes and his accomplices. The terror caused by the Gunpowder Plot gave everybody good grounds for hatred of Catholics and he endorsed the call for strict enforcement of the laws against Recusants and the death penalty for Catholic priests.

His excellent work did not go unnoticed, for the following year he was rewarded by being appointed a judge and he became Chief Justice of the Court of Common Pleas. As he stood in his magnificent scarlet robes and heard the solemn words, 'Well and truly ye shall serve the King and his people. Ye shall take no fee or livery from none but the King', his heart swelled not only with pride, but also with a determination that justice should be unsullied in his hands. He lost none of his arrogance, but he changed almost overnight from a savage prosecutor into a stern but just and un-bribable judge, an almost unheard-of figure in that corrupt and unprincipled period. Thereafter he never wavered in his allegiance to justice which he saw as the cornerstone of the rights and liberties of the ordinary citizen.

If James was particularly interested in some case of law, he would dismiss the judges and take it into his own hands. Sir Edward opposed this constantly, arguing that the King had no power to decide cases himself. 'These should be determined in some court of justice,' he insisted. When the King replied that law was founded on reason and that he and others had reason as well as the judges, Sir Edward boldly replied, 'God hath endowed your Majesty with excellent science and great endowments of nature, but your Majesty is not learned in the laws of the realm of England.' James found this rebuke insufferable.

Not surprisingly, Coke had many enemies, and when one day he stumbled and fell in the presence of the King, the whole court tittered with merriment at his discomfiture. His particular and lifelong opponent was the great philosopher Francis Bacon, who had been an eager suitor for the hand of Lady Elizabeth Hatton and had also hoped for the position of Attorney General when Coke was appointed.

Despite his brilliant reputation, Bacon was desperately short of money, and when his patron, Lord Essex, failed to secure him a position, he gladly accepted a grant of land from him. Later, when Essex fell out of favour, without a flicker of gratitude Bacon happily acted for his prosecution and death sentence and then, unperturbed, accepted a royal pension. Throughout his career he sought royal favour by servility to the Crown with a craven lack of morals. He always upheld the King's prerogative arguing that *Rex est Lex* – the King is the law, holding that difficult cases should of course be decided by James whom he termed 'the most religious learned and judicious King that ever this island had'. Swift summed up Bacon's learning and frailty in his mordant couplet:

'If parts allure thee, think how Bacon shined.
The wisest, brightest, meanest of mankind.'

In 1611 Coke was in trouble when he once again challenged the authority of the Church's disciplinary court, disputing its right to fine and imprison, holding that this was a matter for the law. In order to silence him, James invited Coke to join the Court of High Commission, declaring that he would make some changes to it, ordering Coke and other judges to attend its first meeting. They all obeyed the summons, but Coke refused to sit down until the new constitution had been read out and he resolutely remained standing for some hours throughout the reading. When he found that it contained unacceptable clauses, he refused to be a member of a body which he considered illegal.

In 1613 Bacon became Attorney General and prosecuted

in many cases where Coke was unwilling to find the offender guilty. For example, an elderly and much loved clergyman called Peacham was arrested on the charge of treason for writing a sermon, which he never delivered, saying that in some cases insurrection was justified. Bacon examined him under torture and then, to ensure his conviction, he interviewed each of the judges separately to obtain their co-operation. Coke delivered a stern ruling that 'no commandment or message may be delivered to any of the judges singly'. The unfortunate Peacham died in prison before his trial, but Coke stood stalwartly for justice for the individual, and although such an episode was trivial in itself, in this and many another instances he strengthened the rights of the common man.

As James found him a constant vexation, at Bacon's suggestion he was transferred to be a judge on the King's Bench, where only those matters that directly concerned the Crown were dealt with. The salary was similar and there was a certain cachet in dealing with royal matters, but Coke would no longer judge everyday cases concerning the rights of individual lowly citizens and this was a great sorrow to him. He wept as he received the news, but the King's word in such matters was absolute. Bacon had subtly suggested to James that this promotion would tame Coke and 'he will think himself near a Privy Councillor and turn obsequious instead of obstructing your Majesty's wishes'.

Meeting Bacon shortly afterwards Coke accosted him: 'Mr. Attorney, this is all your doing. It is you that have made this great stir.' And far from denying it, Bacon replied, 'Aha, my Lord, your lordship all this while hath grown in breadth; you must needs grow in height, else you will prove a monster.'

Since the beginning of his legal career, Coke had kept careful notes of every case in which he had been involved and in due course he published these records which laid the foundation of case law. In 1475 Sir Thomas Littleton had written a treatise on Land Tenure and this, with Coke's commentary on it, remained the standard work on land law for generations.

His legal reports brought him nearly as much acclaim as the great philosophical work, Novum Organum, for which Bacon was cited as 'the bell which called the other wits together'. These two great men locked horns, the one learned, unpleasant and arrogant, the other brilliant, servile and amoral, but both immensely beneficial to their country and their age.

In 1613 Coke's daughter Elizabeth was married to Sir Humphrey Berkeley. This was a good match and a great relief to Lady Hatton who had feared her husband's meanness might have prevented him from offering a suitable dowry.

Frances attended her sister's wedding and loved her first incursion into the great and fashionable world. She had a new dress for the occasion and her childish beauty did not go unnoticed, for she was eleven now, with fair golden ringlets and sparkling blue eyes and a most engaging dimple. Her merry laughter and gaiety was infectious and she was the epitome of youthful loveliness – a rosebud. She was intoxicated by all the praise and attention she received, and her mother began to think seriously about a suitable match for such an enchanting child.

To Frances' delight, she began to accompany her mother to the court from time to time. It was lonely for her at Stoke Poges now that Elizabeth was married and she constantly begged her mother to take her with her to London. London was glittering, riotous, exciting. She delighted in the new dresses and jewellery that she now needed to wear for great royal occasions.

On 16th January 1616 there was a special new masque by Ben Johnson, entitled News from the New World, staged to coincide with the visit of the Indian Princess, Pocohontas, who was received most graciously by the King and given a front seat at the play. Few people had ever seen a coloured person before, let alone one who was a princess, and she aroused huge interest, everyone staring at her with disbelief. Frances was presented and made her curtsey to the King and Queen, just as in her childhood dreams, and she met many courtiers, including the handsome haughty George, Viscount Villiers. As a newcomer to court he was disdained by the older families but so loved by James that no-one dared openly criticize his insolent and arrogant behaviour that grew ever more offensive as his intimacy with the King deepened. Indeed, by now anyone wanting a favour or an audience with James knew that their surest path lay through the good graces of George Villiers.

Frances looked up at him timidly as she made her obeisance and saw a young and beautiful man, most radiantly attired, and she blushed as he smiled down at her. A contemporary wrote that he was 'one of the handsomest men in the world; of a kind, free and liberal disposition to them that applied themselves to him, applauded his actions and were wholly his creatures. Wonderfully loving to all his kindred, advancing them all to place and dignity, having the King so tied to him that He would refuse him nothing.'

Sadly for Frances this magical time at court was cut short all too soon when her father annoyed the King yet again and this time there was to be no forgiveness. Once more it was a dispute between the Church and the Law and the subject was a Commendam. This was a process whereby, when a living became vacant, a bishop could hold it vacant indefinitely, taking the profit from it and leaving the parishioners without a priest. Such a case had been brought against the Bishop of Coventry and the judges were hearing it when James sent a peremptory letter to them ordering them not to proceed with the trial. Prompted by Coke, they returned a letter saying that they felt that it was their duty to continue to try the case. James acted swiftly, summoning all the judges to appear before the Council of State. They stood silently before him in their robes in the great Council Chamber as he glared at them in silent anger, then he picked up their letter, tore it into pieces and threw it to the ground. He reminded them severely about his royal prerogative, then required each judge to agree never to hear Commendam cases again. Eleven of them meekly agreed, but Coke replied that he would act as an honest judge should.

For James such opposition was intolerable as he would not allow his authority to be questioned. He tried remonstrance, cajolery and threats, but when all this was to no avail, he pronounced Coke 'impractical' and threatened to remove him from the bench and from all legal duties. Coke received the news with 'tears and great dejection'.

Naturally Bacon was swift to act. He at once sent a letter for the King's signature: 'May it please your Excellent Majestie I send your Majestie a form of discharge for my Lord Coke. I send also a Warrant for making forth a writ for a new Lord Justice, leaving a blank for the name to be supplied by your Majesty's presence, for I never received your Majesty's express pleasure in it.'

Lady Hatton, despite her coolness towards her husband, loyally hurried to the court to plead his case, but unfortunately she was so vehement that she offended the King and, despite the pleas of the Queen and the Prince of Wales, she was told to leave.

People disliked, feared and admired Coke in more or less equal proportions, but everyone enjoyed his discomfiture, so there was a lot of delightfully malicious gossip about the couple and whether or not he would finally be dismissed. On 9th November a correspondent wrote that, 'The Lord Coke hangs in suspense'; and on the 11th there was a flying tale that Lord Villiers' brother John should marry his daughter so that there should be a pacification, and the writer adds of John 'in the meantime he is, as it were, in ague, a good day and a bad by fits'.

Finally on 16th November, Coke received the fatal message signed by the King and sealed with the Great Seal, 'For certain causes moving Us, We will that you shall be no longer be Our Chief Justice to hold place before Us; and We recommend that you no longer interfere in that office. And by virtue of this presence We at once remove and exonerate you from the same.' He and Lady Hatton were banished from the court.

The suggestion that Sir Edward might marry Frances to John Villiers with a little of his land and much more of hers as a dowry so appalled Lady Hatton and caused such friction between them that Sir Edward took temporary refuge with one of his married daughters, a Mistress Sadler, in Norwich. He was far from giving up, despite his heartbreak, for he was so certain that his wisdom was universally acknowledged. Knowing that the King loved hunting and racing, whilst in Norwich he attended Newmarket Races and put himself in the way of the King and kissed his hand. However violent his temper, James never held grudges so he spoke quite kindly to him and was even heard to say of him, 'Wherever you throw that man, he always lands on his legs.'

Despite Lady Hatton's absolute embargo, he continued with his plans to marry Frances to his own advantage. Since reconciliation and forgiveness could only come through the favourite, he approached the Villiers family. George Villiers' mother, thrice married and now Lady Compton, was an ambitious woman and determined that the rest of her children should enjoy some of their brother's good fortune. John, her eldest son, was an unhappy creature, physically unattractive and mentally unstable, suffering such severe bouts of insanity that, from time to time, he had to be banished from court and detained.

Sir Edward negotiated secretly with Lady Compton, offering Frances in marriage to John with the added attraction of a huge dowry, the understanding being that he, Sir Edward, should be restored to favour with the King. Agreement was soon reached and he set off in satisfaction to Stoke Poges.

Lady Hatton was engaged in needlework and Frances was reading to her when the coach drew up outside. They rose to greet Sir Edward and eagerly awaited his news, having had no tidings during his absence, and when he proudly announced that they would all be returning to London shortly to the court, they both expressed their delight and Frances clapped her hands joyfully. He turned to her smiling, saying, 'You will be returning as a bride.' She gasped in disbelief. 'A bride, Sir? A bride to whom? O Father, who is it to be?' He took her hand and paused a moment. 'You will be one of the foremost ladies at court and you will be able to help your family, you will have the ear of the King. We could not have found a more splendid husband for you.' Frances whispered anxiously, 'Who, who, O who?' 'Why, none other than John Villiers, the brother of the favourite himself. You will take precedence over most ladies of the court, even over your own mother.' 'No, no. No!' Frances shuddered. 'He is horrible, he laughs like a maniac. No, no!'

She broke down in hysterical tears and turned to her mother. Lady Hatton put her arm around Frances and declared that she should never marry such a low-born half-wit. Sir Edward curtly told them that his orders were not to be questioned and he commanded them to prepare for the wedding. He then left them and returned to London.

They sat awhile in deep grief, Lady Hatton holding the sobbing Frances in her arms; then she rose and ordered her coach. Half an hour later, mother and daughter had fled.

Fugitives

T hey did not go very far. Their destination was Oatlands Park, the home of a cousin of Lady Elizabeth, only about fifteen miles away, but as they left in the afternoon, darkness was soon upon them. Frances was still trembling and holding tightly to her mother's arm as they bumped up and down on the uneven roads, travelling swiftly away from Stoke Poges, but all too soon, in fading light, they had to slow first to a trot, then to walking pace as the horses started to stumble in the twilight, whilst Lady Hatton constantly urged the coachman to hasten.

Mercifully the moon appeared and aided them, although its light cast strange eerie shadows from the swaying branches of the trees lining the roadway. It was nearing dawn when the travellers arrived, cold, tired and anxious, and to their dismay found that the house was empty with the shutters closed.

'Rouse the steward' ordered Lady Hatton peremptorily and they remained shivering in the coach for what seemed an interminable delay until the steward appeared with a cloak hastily thrown over his nightshirt and his eyes all bleary with sleep. He explained unhappily that Sir William was away on the continent and would not return for some months, but when he saw and recognized Lady Hatton, who was a relation and frequent guest in his master's house, he was quick to assure them that Sir William would be happy for them to stay.

Negotiations were short, as Lady Hatton insisted on absolute secrecy – indeed, she explained, it was good that the house was shut and the staff were absent as they would require only one servant who must be absolutely trustworthy and discreet.

The following morning they had the locks reinforced on all the doors, the windows were barred and they hardly left the house, barely venturing into the garden in case they should be seen and their presence reported. At first Frances remained shocked and tearful, begging her mother again and again to promise that she should never marry John Villiers and to this her mother gladly agreed. There was no sign of trouble the next day, and when a week passed peacefully, Frances grew gradually calmer and even began to enjoy the adventure, helping with the cooking, picking the vegetables and exploring every inch of the house.

Lady Hatton, on the contrary, grew ever more concerned, because she knew only too well that they could not hope to remain concealed forever and there was only one solution. Frances must be married or at least affianced to someone else and then neither Sir Edward nor the King himself could undo a marriage vow – gone were all her great plans for a glittering court wedding, and all she could hope for now was to find someone of good family, sound in body and mind. Money was less important for she, Lady Hatton, could provide a dowry.

She finally decided to approach a distant relative, Henry de Vere, Earl of Oxford. He was unfortunately abroad, so she could not contact him in person, but she forged a letter purporting to come from him containing an offer of marriage. She showed this to Frances and made her write a formal acceptance. She then wrote to the young man, explaining matters and never doubting but that he would be happy to accept such a beautiful and well-endowed bride. Thereafter all she could do was wait, but as the days turned into weeks, she quaked with fear each time she heard horses.

When Sir Edward returned to Stoke Poges, expecting that the wedding preparations would be well under way, and he learnt of their disappearance, he was beside himself with rage. He savagely questioned all the servants, but they finally convinced him that they had no knowledge of the whereabouts of the fugitives, only that the coach had left shortly after he had returned to London. He sent out scouts in every direction and made enquiries of every local justice of the peace, but as the days passed and he failed to find their hiding place, so his anger increased. It offended him personally to have a wife who was disobedient, and it was also a breach of the law, which held that it was his legal right to marry his daughter to whomsoever he wished. Worse still, he knew that he was the butt and laughing stock of the court and most of London, all of whom enjoyed the whole affair hugely; but perhaps most serious of all, he felt anxious that too much delay and opposition might cause the Villiers family to withdraw the offer and so impede his return to favour.

It was six full weeks before he discovered the hiding place and then he lost no time. He put on his breast plate and took out his pistols, he summoned one of his sons by his first marriage, a wild young man nicknamed Fighting Clem, and with a small posse of retainers, he set out for Oatlands.

It was dusk when they arrived, circled the house and tethered their horses. There was no sign of life, the doors were stout and well barred and there was no answer to their repeated knocking, so they prowled around shouting ferociously to frighten the women and banging on the casements. For a while they wondered whether they would ever be successful without battering down the doors, but at last one of the party saw a tiny unbarred window hidden by ivy and through this they were able to force an entrance.

Inside all was dark and utterly silent and they had no idea whether or how it might be defended, so Sir Edward called out, 'If you kill us, it will be illegal and murder, but if we harm you, it will be justifiable because you are disobeying the law.' He ordered every one of his party to shout loudly, so that the fugitives would believe that there was a large number of intruders.

By the light of tapers and lanterns, they began to search the house systematically room by room and floor by floor which took a long time, but at last in the attic at the top of the house they found their quarry – mother and daughter – cowering terrified in a tiny cupboard. They were dragged out none too gently and Lady Hatton screamed in anger and defiance as Frances was torn from her arms and carried outside to Clem's horse. He put her roughly before him and held her tightly as they galloped off, leaving her mother behind raging at them. They took the precaution of sawing through the axle of her coach, leaving her a virtual prisoner.

For Frances it was a terrifying and painful ride. Clem's arms held her round her waist in front of him. She was bruised by the front of the saddle and the reins cut into her side and she tried to slip to the ground, but Clem held her too fast. The first gallop was fearsome, but when they slowed to a trot, the discomfort was even greater and she felt battered all over. She cried to him in her pain, but he only laughed. For mile after mile and hour after hour she endured what felt like unremitting torture, but at last they arrived back at Stoke Poges, riding through the familiar gates and up the drive. Outside the front door, Clem laughed and relaxed his grip and she fell to the ground, only to hear her father's curt tones to his servant. 'Take the lady upstairs to the oak room, lock the door and bring me the key.' Then he turned to Frances who was still on the ground, 'Do as I say or you will be carried there.'

Painfully she struggled to her feet, moved towards her father and started to speak, but he merely turned away, telling the groom to see to the horses. Seeing that resistance was useless, she slowly mounted the stairs and entered the attic room, bruised in body and fearful in mind, and as she heard the key turn in the lock, she fell down on the bed, sobbing, bewildered and forlorn.

She slept very little, but when morning dawned, she determined to beg her father once more not to force her into this marriage. She felt he could not condemn her to marry anyone so abhorrent. She had seen John Villiers at court, indeed it was hard not to notice him, he looked so strange, with a high maniacal laugh, and her father must have seen this too. She had noticed people mocking him behind his back when his brother was not there, and the mere thought that he might kiss her made her tears flow again.

She was hungry now and thirsty, but she had neither food nor water – she could not even wash her tear-stained face and still no-one came near her. She began to panic and wondered whether they would leave her here to starve, and although she cried out and beat the door with her fists, all was silent.

She could tell by the sun that it was midday before she heard footsteps on the stairs, and as she rose from the bed her heart beat faster, but she still resolved to beg for mercy. As the key turned she moved towards the door, and then saw with dismay that it was neither her father, nor even her stepbrother, Clem, but a shame-faced servant who stood there bearing a tray with a glass of water and a piece of bread.

'Alfred,' she begged, 'where is my father?' He pushed the tray towards her in embarrassment. 'The master has gone to London', he stammered uncomfortably, 'and we aren't nohow allowed to speak to you – and Mr. Clem is downstairs listening,' he added hastily by way of explanation. Alfred had known Frances all her life and it grieved him to see her treated this way, but his fear of Sir Edward was too great for him to disobey. He pushed the platter towards her and hastily left, closing and locking the door securely behind him.

She drank the water eagerly and began to understand just how determined her father was. He was not to be swayed, and now all her hopes must rest on her mother who had promised that the marriage should never take place. She would surely keep that promise.

Monotonous days passed. She was given little food, nobody was allowed to speak to her and her father never appeared, so she had no chance to appeal to him for mercy. She had nothing to read; she searched every corner of the room, hoping to find something, anything to occupy her and ease her tedium and terrible loneliness; she studied the hanging curtain and looked at the birds embroidered on it and longed for wings. The window was barred, so there was no hope of escape there, but she spent much of her time looking out and wondering whether she dared call out for help if she saw anyone passing by. Her face grew thinner, her cheeks became paler, and her unhappiness grew with every passing day.

Meanwhile Lady Hatton, although only slightly bruised in body, was outraged in mind, incensed by the rough manhandling she had received; her pride was wounded by her husband's behaviour and she became more determined than ever that the marriage should never take place. It was some little time before she was able to summon help and get her coach repaired, but as soon as she could she set out for London and went straight to her husband's enemy, Sir Francis Bacon, where she felt sure of a sympathetic hearing. When she arrived, the doorkeeper informed her that My Lord Keeper was ill in bed, asleep at present and far too unwell to receive anyone. Lady Hatton, quite undeterred, persuaded him to lodge her in a room adjacent to Bacon's, whereupon she began to beat upon the walls so loudly that Bacon was alarmed and shouted for help and, as the servants hurried to his aid, she rushed in with them like a cow that has lost its calf.

She complained of assault and battery and demanded an injunction against her husband which Sir Francis most happily granted, and it was with pleasure that he agreed to summon Coke to the Star Chamber. He espoused her cause eagerly and offered to communicate with the King and George Villiers on her behalf. As unfortunately they happened to be away together on a visit to Scotland, Sir Francis wrote to them immediately and at length, strongly advising against a match with a family in disgrace, moreover one in which religion and Christian discretion was disliked, and he humbly offered his help and his services in the affair.

To his surprise and chagrin, he got exceedingly cool replies from both the King and George Villiers. Villiers wrote, 'In this bisynes of my brother's that you overtrouble yourself with, I understand from London that you have carryed yourself with much scorn and neglect both towards my selfe and my friends.' It was a menacing letter, but the one from the King was no better. James wrote that to take sides with a wife against her husband was to be in league with Delilah and he added, 'Whereas you talk of the riot and violence committed by Sir Edward Coke we wonder you make no mention of the riot and violence of them that stole away his daughter, which was the first ground of all that noise.'

Bacon was so much alarmed by the antagonism he had aroused that he quickly disclaimed disapproval of the match, assuring the King and Villiers that he was only anxious to be of assistance in any way he could. He quickly ceased to press Lady Hatton's cause.

Sir Edward Coke, skilful lawyer that he was, went to Winwood, the Chief Secretary, and laid serious charges against his wife – namely that she had abducted his child and attempted to marry her without his consent, both of which were unlawful. Finally he accused her of the serious crime of perjury in that she had forged a letter purporting it to have been written by the Earl of Oxford.

The court, which had thoroughly enjoyed the preliminary skirmish a couple of months before, settled down to hear the sequel, some holding that women should be kept in their rightful place and that Sir Edward's sharp treatment of his wife was a salutary lesson to be applauded by all heads of household, yet no-one loved the Villiers and this latest attempt to enrich and ennoble themselves by marrying the feeble-minded elder brother to a young and beautiful child was felt by some to be outrageous.

A contemporary letter testifies to the general enjoyment of the affair. 'I hear nothing so much spoken of as that of Sir John Villiers and Sir Edward Coke's daughter. My Lady Hatton doth continue stiff against yt.'

A few weeks later, the King returned from Scotland with George Villiers and he happily agreed to arbitrate on the matter, for this was the sort of family skirmish that he loved, feeling that he was the wise father and kindly overseer of court and courtiers. Needless to say, the King upheld Sir Edward, believing as he did in a husband's absolute authority over his wife, but more importantly, he was incensed by the slight to his beloved George, feeling that everybody should be honoured to marry into the Villiers family.

Frances woke up one morning in her prison room to learn that she was to be moved that day, but her first feeling of relief was quickly dampened by the news that she was now to be committed to the care of her mother-in-law-to-be, Lady Compton, in order for her – according to the slightly sinister directive – 'to winne and to weare'. It was later said of her that she 'discherished' her daughter-in-law and certainly this was no happy start to their relationship.

When Lady Compton began to discuss the wedding, Frances declared indignantly that she would never marry John, whereupon she was accused of gross impertinence and Lady Compton declared that such behaviour must be punished. When Frances repeated her refusal to the marriage with John, she was tied to the bedpost and whipped with a birch, and although she wept and protested and screamed with pain when the cane cut into her shoulders, there was no pity for her. Her back was scarred with weals and bruising as day after day the ill treatment was repeated. She was starved and beaten until at last she could hold out no more.

As a last resource she declared that she could not legally marry without her mother's consent and she was then allowed to see her father who dictated a letter for her to send to her mother. At his behest she wrote a piteous little missive:

'Madam, I must now humbly desire your patience in giving me leave to declare myself unto you, which is that without your allowance and liking, all the world shall never make me entangle or tie myself. But now by my father's special commandment, I obey him in presenting to you my humble duty in a tedious letter, which is to know your Ladyship's pleasure, not as a thing I desire, but I resolve to be wholly ruled by my father and yourself, knowing your judgement to be such that I may well rely on, I being a mere child and not understanding the world, nor what is good for me. That which makes me a little give way is that it will be a means to procure a reconciliation between my father and your Ladyship. Also I think it will be a means of the King's favour to my father. Himself is not to be disliked, a gentleman well born, so I humbly take my leave. Your Ladyship's most humble and obedient daughter for ever. Dear Mother, believe there has been no violent means used against me by word or deed.'

Once the letter had been dispatched, Frances' spirits lifted a little for Lady Compton assured her that after agreeing to the marriage, subject to her mother's consent, there would be no further persuasion, and as she had her mother's most faithful promise, all would now be well. She would be allowed to return home and the whole objectionable business would be forgotten.

Unknown to Frances, Lady Hatton had already been apprehended at her husband's request and with Bacon's assistance, and as was customary with noble ladies, she was not in prison, but in close custody at the house of Sir William Craven, where she was unable to pursue Frances' cause. Sir Francis Bacon, now thoroughly frightened by the King's obvious displeasure and Villiers' open hostility, urgently begged her to agree to the marriage.

Lord Oxford had returned from abroad, but showed no inclination to intervene and it was assumed that 'although it would have been a great fortune for my Lord, yet it is doubtful whether he would endanger the loss of the King's favour, even for 'so fayre a woman and so fayre a fortune'.

Lady Hatton was in despair, held in close confinement with no freedom to get in touch with anyone who might have helped her, and she was painfully aware of the attitude of the King and of George Villiers knowing that Frances' marriage lay in their power. Her husband had already been re-admitted to the court and to audience with the King and Queen, whereas serious charges had now been laid by him against her and he was pressing for her prosecution. She was contemptuous of this and unafraid of any legal consequences, but Sir Edward now coldly assured her that if she refused her consent to this match, no other nobleman would dare to step forward and Frances could never wed at all. She was condemning her daughter to spinsterhood or a convent because of her personal disdain for the Villiers. She must realize, he argued, that this marriage would bring them all great distinction, that she would be closely related to the King's favourite, that their daughter could become important in the constant struggle for the King's favour and she knew only too well just how much Frances enjoyed life at court with parties and jewels and fine clothes, so she must decide on the child's fate – spinsterhood or marriage to John Villiers. It was an intolerable situation and she delayed and prevaricated, but finally, in deepest despair, she gave her reluctant consent.

When Frances was given this news by an exultant Lady Compton, she at first refused to believe it, but was given little time to grieve, for the wedding date was already fixed and approaching and she was taken to her uncle's house at Richmond to prepare. It was to be a great occasion, to be held on 28th September at Hampton Court where the ceremony would be conducted by the Bishop of Winchester in the presence of the King and Queen and everyone of note.

Although there were 700 rooms at Hampton Court, the entire space between the river and the palace was filled with tents for servants and lesser persons who were unable to find space inside. Most guests arrived by barge and the Thames was filled with jostling rivercraft, nobody wanting to miss this magnificent affair and some even wondering whether the unhappy bride might dare to rebel at the last moment.

For Frances the day started early when her father fetched her from her uncle's house to take her to Hampton Court. He took great care handing her into the coach so that her dress might remain faultless; this confused and frightened her for never before had he treated her with such decorum, almost as if she were already a great lady. She wore a gown of white brocade, her fair hair hung down in ringlets held by a single band of silver set with pearls and diamonds and a gossamer veil hid her face. She had numbly allowed herself to be dressed by her aunt's maid who had petted and comforted her and tried to dry the tears that flowed all too steadily.

At first they drove in silence and she listened to the sound of the horses' trotting as they drew her ever nearer to the dreaded moment. Then Sir Edward took her arm and told her gently that now she would be one of the first ladies in the land, and save for marrying the great George Villiers himself, he and her mother could never have arranged a better match for her; she was no longer a child and she must now play her part in helping her family to greatness; her possibilities were limitless.

Frances felt a stab of pain at the mention of her mother – even until now she had hoped for her intervention, and she knew that she could never forgive her for her broken promise. Just once during the journey she ventured to stammer a word of her unwillingness and her father's manner changed abruptly. Yes, of course she could decline, but the alternative would be life in a strict convent where escape would be impossible and silence perpetual. A sigh and a little sob escaped her and she said no more.

After that everything happened with a dreadful swift inevitability. The coach drew up close to the chapel entrance and she could hear the sound of triumphant music greeting their entrance at the porch. The chapel was full to overflowing, the loud murmur of voices suddenly ceased and it was in profound silence that Sir Edward, proud in his black breeches and finely bejewelled coat, his head held high as if to emphasize his return to favour, walked slowly towards the altar, whilst on his arm there drooped the slender figure of his daughter. Frances felt as if her legs would give way under her and she clutched her father's arm for fear of falling.

During the long slow procession up the aisle, she was too numb to be conscious of the throng of guests, unaware of the interested gaze of the congregation, some pitying, some merely curious. She could not stop a sob escaping her from time to time and her tears flowed so freely that more than once she had to raise her hand beneath her veil to wipe her wet cheeks.

At the altar steps stood John and his brother George, and then the King himself stepped forward and took Frances' arm to give her away, and at this signal honour Sir Edward gave a deferential bow and withdrew. The Bishop, resplendent in robes and mitre, began the service and Frances was too overawed by the solemnity of the occasion even to consider rebellion and she meekly whispered the responses as in a nightmare.

The ceremony was followed by a magnificent banquet at which Frances sat at the King's side, whilst her bridegroom stood behind her chair. Her brother-in-law, George, sat next to her and all around sat the great officers of state. King James, who loved a family occasion, drank freely, kissed Frances repeatedly, proposed the young couple's health and reiterated his love for the Villiers. 'I love the Villiers family above all people,' he asserted repeatedly. It was a long drawn-out meal of many platters and much drink, but Frances could hardly eat and felt that she would surely choke as the King plied her with food and drink. She kept thinking with terror of what was yet to come.

Finally she found herself being undressed by unknown hands, accompanied by many a sickeningly bawdy joke, then she was attired in a white shift and propelled with much laughter towards the great bridal bed where John and the King were waiting. James tickled the terrified Frances then himself tucked them up, drew the bed curtains and bade them stay there until he called them in the morning. The noise and shouting subsided, the door was shut and there was a sudden and frightening silence.

In despair after this long and horrible day which had been one blur of misery, Frances' body stiffened in apprehension. John was gentle. He wiped away her tears and put his arm around her to draw her closer towards him. She gave a little cry of pain, for her shoulders still bore the scars, as yet unhealed, from the many whippings she had suffered. 'Do I hurt you?' he asked. In an explosion of grief, she wept inconsolably and told him, in between her sobs, of all the beatings and starvation that had forced her to this marriage. 'Perhaps no one would marry me unless they were forced to,' he said bitterly, then added, 'Frances, I loved you from the first time I saw you and I always will. Perhaps one day, you will come to love me a little.' He kissed her bruised shoulders and bade her sleep. 'We shall have a lifetime together – tomorrow I shall make you my wife.'

Frances lay quietly, relieved and surprised, yet still anxious. She had heard lurid stories of the rough treatment a bride might expect on her wedding night, yet John had been unexpectedly kind and in a few moments she heard his breathing grow steadier and realized that he was already asleep. She did not sleep, but lay awake for many hours wondering about this strange man who was now her wedded lord, who assured her that he loved her and who yet went to sleep like a child on his wedding night. She could feel no affection for John and his body repelled her, yet she was moved by his gentleness and his declaration of love for her.

She dreaded the next day which would bring stares and innuendoes and bawdy jibes, particularly from the King, which she must perforce endure in patience. But above all, she knew that she would never ever forgive her mother for breaking her promise and giving her consent to this unwelcome marriage. Without her betrayal it could not have taken place.

Marriage

Frances woke early after fitful sleep and listened to John's measured breathing beside her, but when she gently pulled back the heavy bed hanging she found that day was breaking and there was the sound of scurrying footsteps outside. She hesitated awhile, remembering the King's admonition that they were not to move until he called them, and she wondered whether that was mere banter or if he had meant it.

She shrank from meeting the crowd of wedding guests, fearing the King's bawdy tongue and unwelcome jocularity, but her problems were solved when John's personal servant knocked loudly at the door and announced that the King had decided that the court was to return to Whitehall that morning. Thereafter, such was the turmoil that nobody even considered the bridal pair.

John rose and allowed himself to be dressed, but he was clearly excited and kept laughing alarmingly and unnecessarily. Frances was thankful for the bustle and

confusion as they hastened towards the river where one of the
Villiers' barges awaited them; she was deeply embarrassed
as to what John might say or do next. Thankfully they drew
away almost unnoticed and she sighed with relief, but she
thought bitterly of her childhood dreams about life at court
as the wife of a young and winsome husband, whereas now
she was miserably bound to someone unattractive, unstable
and despised by all.

Although no-one would ever dare openly criticize the
brother of the King's favourite, she was well aware of
the whispers, sniggers, sudden silences, odd remarks and
a certain ostracism of them both. By birth and preference
she belonged to the old court circle, but by marriage she
was now classed amongst the unwelcome Villiers, yet
none of the Villiers showed her any affection except for
poor afflicted John. She found his devotion to her deeply
perplexing, something which she could not reciprocate,
nor yet as her wedded husband could she turn away from
him. She had to appear on his arm each day and in her
bitterness she vowed over and over again that she would
never forgive her mother.

At first they did not need to meet. Lady Hatton had been
invited to the wedding, but she had refused and remained
as if in confinement. A week or two later, the Villiers
together with many others, twelve coaches in all, set off to
bring her back from Sir William Craven's custody where

she was said to be 'crazy in body and sick in mind'. They took her to recuperate at Cecil House, her father's home, whilst Sir Edward still continued to urge her prosecution for conspiracy, disobedience and perjury.

The King, having championed the match, now endeavoured to bring peace all round. Urged on by Lady Compton, he suggested that Lady Hatton, perhaps to compensate for her obduracy, should give her daughter the lands around Purbeck, but this she refused to do. 'For aught I hear, the Lady Hatton holds her hands and gives not her milk as freely as was expected' wrote a contemporary.

James then decided that, although they might not have the lands, or at least not yet, John and Frances should have the title, so he created John Viscount Purbeck and Frances found herself with the dignity of Viscountess. John was appointed Master of Horse to Prince Charles and the couple were given official lodgings in Denmark House. Since his beloved George must always have precedence, the King now made him Earl of Buckingham, and his mother was given the courtesy title of Countess of Buckingham.

James was free with titles. Before his accession, there were just sixty-one noble families, all of ancient lineage and mostly interrelated, and these made up the court circle.

There were about six hundred knights, most of whom lived in the shires and served as justices and local administrators. In one single year, when the King was hard up, he invented the new title of Baronet and created two hundred, each one paying one thousand pounds for the privilege. Even James was a little shamefaced about this, but Lord Cecil, his Chancellor, reassured him saying, 'Tush Sire, you need the money. That will do you good and it will do them very little harm.'

Having seen that the young couple were provided for, James would have liked to have made peace between Sir Edward and his wife, but when urged to make up with her husband, Lady Hatton declared, although almost certainly not directly to the King, that she would rather make friends with the devil. She never lived with him again, but she yearned above all for her daughter's forgiveness and that was not forthcoming. When she finally accepted that she could not un-do the knot and she must accept the marriage, she crept back to court with little state but was greeted well by the King who reconciled her with the Queen and made an atonement between her and the newly-ennobled Countess of Buckingham.

According to James, he finally concluded a perfect peace betwixt Lady Hatton and her daughter, who would not be persuaded to forgive and forget until, at the end of an evening of merriment, Lady Hatton begged the King to make Frances swear that she loved her as dearly as she ever had in her life. As this was at the behest of the King, Frances had little choice, but a promise so exacted did nothing to change her feelings.

However, the everyday regime at Westminster meant that they inevitably met. Lady Hatton celebrated her return to favour by giving a most magnificent feast which she insisted that Frances attend, and she and Frances stood behind the King's chair. It was said that 'the King graced her in every way and made two of her creatures knights, but the principal graces and favours fell on the Countess of Buckingham and her children, whom the King praised, and kissed and blessed all those that wished them well.' The report continues: 'There were some errors at Lady Hatton's feast (if it were not done on purpose) but the greatest was the absence of Lord Coke who had to eat a solitary dinner elsewhere.'

Frances had no alternative but to settle down with John and join in life at Whitehall which was a round of bawdy merriment and gossip and tittle-tattle and not a little evil conniving, as everyone strove to stand well with the King and his favourite. Daily life at Whitehall did not start early, as everyone dressed with great care and elegance, advertising their wealth with precious jewellery and costly raiment. At noon they lunched, after which they might row on the river, watch bear baiting or cock fighting and on every event bets were laid, often for ridiculously large sums. Crafty courtiers such as Lord Dorset always contrived to let the King's cocks win and made his money with less important owners. The courtiers sometimes visited the play house, where they vexed the 'groundlings', or common people, by sitting on the stage and spoiling their view of the actors. Around 4 o'clock they dined, and frequently there were masques, balls, water pageants and individual feasts. At 9 o'clock, if there were no festivities, everyone assembled for the ceremony of the King going to bed and vied with each other to be near the royal person and speak with him.

Shortly after Lady Hatton's feast, Lord Buckingham also entertained the King and as it was given for a very special purpose, it was called the 'friends' peace'. There had been a ferocious argument between Buckingham and Prince Charles, in which Buckingham was so far gone in arrogance that he told the Prince to kiss his arse and even attempted to strike him – a truly heinous offence. James patched up the quarrel between the two young men and then, unbelievably, he declared himself for his beloved favourite.

In the same room where the King dined was a separate table for the lords and ladies, and the Countess of Buckingham, Lady Hatton and Frances, now described as John Villiers' Lady, were among those present. The King honoured them by drinking to them in particular, one after the other, and at the end of dinner he rose and came personally to their table and drank a common health. This was a most unusual honour and James surely did his best to bring them together, but to little avail. Frances had reached the court, she saw the King and Queen frequently and they were gracious to her, she had a royal apartment and a lofty title, but how empty and uninviting this all seemed. The excitement unhinged John's poor mind and from time to time his behaviour became so bizarre that he had to be removed from court until he recovered somewhat.

There was much correspondence about John's behaviour, and a letter from Lord Conway says, 'His Majestie prays you not to thinke it a little distemper which carryed him to these publique actes and publique places which may and must reflect upon his most noble brother', adding almost surely in the King's own words that if anything dire were to happen, 'there cannot bee soe much a 'whoe would have thought it', which is the foules answer, as a distempered minde may doe the worst to be done', and a reluctant Sir John Hippisley was put in charge of him.

Her mother-in-law was swift to blame Frances for all John's ills of mind and body. His malady was periodic – he swung from deep depression when he would weep in her arms to a climax of rowdy and impossible behaviour, when he would be taken away until he improved.

It was not easy for a lady to attend court functions without a husband or a male chaperone, least of all a bride of fifteen, and Frances often found herself deeply embarrassed and anxious or unhappily alone. She could not love her strange husband, but she pitied him deeply and she was always gentle and patient with him, while his devotion to her was absolute and enduring.

She had no option but to face life at Whitehall with or without John, but about this time, it seemed, she had a stroke of good fortune when her cousin, Elizabeth Cecil, married Thomas Howard, the eldest son of the Earl of Suffolk. The two young brides enjoyed each other's company and began to meet almost every day. The Suffolks had six sons, and the fifth, Robert, although much the same age as John, was so very different – merry, handsome, well born and altogether delightful. At the age of thirteen Frances had watched him with admiration when she first came to court with her mother and she had been present at the great celebration when Prince Charles was created Prince of Wales and Robert and his younger brother William had been knighted. Robert had brown hair, which he wore shoulder length, and grey green eyes, which sparkled as he smiled. Frances soon realized that it was usually Robert who stood ready to give her an arm into the barge when they sailed, and after a while his arm held her a little longer than was really necessary and she found that she did not draw away. Robert contrived to sit beside her at the dining table – in short he became a devoted admirer and a constant companion. He was Member of Parliament for Bishop's Castle, but as James seldom summoned Parliament, he was usually present at the court. Naturally everybody loved gossip, be it good or, even better, be it injurious, and it was not long before there were vague rumours about Frances that 'in her desolation of heart, she turned to Robert, a noble youth'.

The year 1617 was famous for a brilliant comet which was visible all over England. People riding at night described it like 'a great canopie in the sky' and many feared that it was an evil omen, foretelling disaster, perhaps even the end of the world. Belief in witchcraft and magic was widespread, and the King himself was fearful of the supernatural and issued an edict against it early in his reign, saying that 'if any person shall exercise, consult, employ, feed or reward any evil or wicked spirit or take up any man, woman or child out of the grave to be used in any manner of enchantment, sorcery or witchcraft, whereby any person shall be killed, destroyed, wasted, consumed, pined or lamed, every such offender, their aides, abettors and counsellors shall suffer the pain of death.'

Despite this, in the year of the comet, soothsayers, fortune tellers and astrologers abounded and were very popular. Frances decided to visit one herself, hoping perhaps that he might foretell some future happiness. Robert gladly accompanied her and they were ushered into a darkened room, lit only by the eerie red flames of a brazier. This gave off an intoxicating scent of incense, and the rising smoke cast strange shadows on the walls which were decorated with skulls and crossbones and the signs of the zodiac. The notorious fortune teller Dr. Lambe, himself stood to receive them, his arms outstretched, wearing a tunic with long winged sleeves. It was an unnerving experience. Frances sadly learnt nothing to comfort her, but her visit did not go unnoticed and was duly reported to her mother-in-law.

The following year, 1618, saw a great public outcry at the execution of Sir Walter Raleigh. He was greatly loved and Lord Carew spent a good while upon his knees before the King to plead his case, but His Majesty held that it was as good to hang him here as to deliver him to the King of Spain, who certainly would. This was inevitable if the case were as the Spanish ambassador Gondomar had represented it. Sir Lewis Stucley was sent to apprehend Sir Walter and was promptly renamed Sir Judas Stucley. The Earl of Nottingham was so incensed that he addressed him, 'Thou base fellow, thou scorn and contempt of man. You are saucy to come into my presence.' Sir Lewis at once complained to the King, but all the reply he got was, 'Wouldst thou have me hang him? Upon my soul if I should hang all that speak ill of thee, all the trees in England would not suffice.'

The following year the Queen died. There was not sufficient money for a fitting funeral, so she lay in state for two months. Her ladies-in-waiting took it in turns to keep vigil by her bier and Lady Hatton was amongst them. She walked in the funeral cortege, where each lady wore a gown made of 16 yards of black cloth which so weighed them down that they could barely walk. She was truly grieved, not only because of her personal affection for the Queen, but also because now she had no immediate access to the royal circle, and she was ever anxious for Frances because of the overt hostility that the Villiers showed towards her.

The year 1520 proved disastrous for the family. Shortly after the Queen's funeral, Lady Hatton's father, Lord Cecil, died, and in deep grief she retired to Corfe Castle to mourn alone, away from the busy bustling court.

Sir Edward had only partially got back into favour. He returned to the Privy Council, but he was not returned to the bench; he was asked to serve on many important committees and he was widely expected to become the next Lord Chancellor, the post he had always coveted, and most lawyers, knowing him to be a just and fearless judge, fervently hoped for his appointment, but he was passed over. When the position of Lord Treasurer become vacant, he was thought to be the most likely candidate for the post, but he was only made one of several Commissioners of the Treasury. Rumours abounded that he was to be ennobled, but that never occurred. He said of himself that he was 'tossed up and down like a tennis ball'. It was almost certainly owing to his own unbending attitude that promotion eluded him, for he never ceased to vex the King, whilst Bacon continued to flatter James and agree with him.

In Parliament Coke spoke strongly against Spain and above all against a marriage contract between Charles and the Spanish Infanta who was a Catholic, declaring, 'It is true that the father, even amongst private men, should have power to marry his children, but may we petition the King how his prerogative is to be exercised for the public good ... he ought to marry the Prince to one of his own religion. On such matters the greatest princes have taken the advice of parliament. Edward III did confer with the Commons about his own marriage. The very writ of summons shows that we are called hither to advise for the defence and state of the King and Kingdom.' James found this breathtakingly impertinent and was not slow to reply. 'This plenipotency of yours invests you in all power upon earth, lacking nothing but the Pope's, to have the keys also of heaven and purgatory. Concerning the match of our dearest son, we desire to know how you could presume to determine in that point without committing high treason.' His message continued: 'Make known to the House that none therein shall henceforth presume to meddle with any thing concerning our government or deep matters of state. We think Ourselves very free and able to punish any man's misdemeanour in Parliament as well during the sitting as after.'

To James' fury and dismay, his threat was answered by a Protestation which declared that 'the liberties, franchises, privileges and jurisdictions of Parliament are the ancient and undoubted birthright and inheritance of the subjects of England, and the affairs concerning the King, state and defence of the realm are proper subjects for parliament and every member of the House hath freedom of speech and every member of the House hath like freedom from all impeachment, imprisonment and molestation.'

His anger exploded when he realized that as speaker Coke was the initiator of this document. It was an act of great courage on Sir Edward's part and just one more occasion when he asserted and defended the rights and privileges of Parliament against an increasingly autocratic and angry monarch.

'We are an old and experienced King and We will not suffer that our power be questioned,' he fulminated. He ordered the Protestation to be brought to Whitehall and, before the sight of the Privy Council, he tore the document into shreds and dissolved Parliament.

He arrested Coke and some others whom he termed the 'turbulent party', and Sir Edward found himself in a cold dark cell in the Fleet Prison, at first denied pen, paper or candles. The Fleet Prison stood on the banks of the Fleet

River, close to its confluence with the Thames, a sluggish ditch full of rubbish. Dead animals floated on its surface and butchers' offal contributed to its stench. Occasionally it was cleared so that barges might come up to Holborn Bridge, but it quickly filled up again. The prison walls were many feet thick and light only entered by narrow slits, so the rooms were dark, dank and gloomy. Coke was forbidden to see any of his friends, servants or relations, and all his rooms were searched and all papers taken from his chambers in the Temple, but he was far too wise for anything incriminating to be found.

In his miserable prison he received a bitter, anonymous letter, probably penned by Bacon, accusing him of pride and arrogance, assuring him of the wholesomeness of affliction, and suggesting he should see his errors: 'You speak too much, your affections are entangled with a love of your own arguments, you cloy your audiences, you converse with books and not with men. If you converse, then but with underlings, ever to teach, never to learn. Your too much love of the world is too much seen, when having the income of £10,000, you relieve few or none, the hand that hath taken so much, can it give so little.' The letter ends commending Coke to God's Holy Spirit. It was a cruel letter to one already in deep distress. Presently he was allowed writing materials and he busied himself by writing up the legal reports for which he became famous. He passed seven long months in that dismal dungeon.

In order for his imprisonment to be justified, several charges were brought against him, suggesting that there were inaccuracies in his law reports, that he had not paid debts from Sir William Hatton's will, and most curious of all, that he had allowed his coachman to appear bareheaded. In due course these were all dismissed, but he realized sadly that he would never now achieve high office. His humiliation was completed when his rival, Bacon, had years of triumph, becoming Lord Chancellor and being elevated to the peerage as Lord St. Albans, and publishing his great philosophical work Novem Organum. On the cover there was a picture of the ship of learning and he sent a copy to Sir Edward Coke, who looked at it and remarked, 'It deserveth not to be read in scholes, but rather to be freighted in the ship of foules.'

When he was released, Coke returned to Parliament and resumed his vigorous opposition to any infringements of its power. The following year, he had the satisfaction of seeing Bacon's impeachment for taking bribes. His plea of guilty found him sentenced to imprisonment, and he received a heavy fine and was banished from holding further office, but his plea of guilty exonerated Coke from pressing charges, and a contemporary wrote of Coke 'he would die if he could not help to ruin a great man once in seven years', so no doubt he relished Bacon's downfall. He had two later moments of great glory in Parliament, firstly when he dared to mention Buckingham by name as the cause of their troubles and everyone in the chamber echoed 'T'is he, t'is he'. Parliament was instantly prorogued, but the accusation had been made. And some years later, in the reign of Charles I, he was concerned with the great Petition of Rights, the first statutory restriction on the prerogative of the crown, an enormous step for the rights of the individual.

New Arrangements

With her father in prison and her mother still grieving in Corfe Castle, the Villiers family began to blame Frances openly for John's mental breakdowns. She was seventeen now – lonely, lovely and deeply unhappy.

At last when John's behaviour once more became unacceptable, Buckingham intervened and shut him up in the newly-acquired family home, Wallingford House. Poor John did his utmost to escape by breaking a window, but he only managed to cut himself and he was discovered covered in blood. This episode established the family's opinion that he was seriously ill and needed protection.

Buckingham took control of all John's estate, including Frances' dowry, her jewels, her clothes and her household stuff and shut her out of Denmark House. She returned home one day to find her apartment empty and locked.

With courage prompted by despair, Frances decided to go herself to Wallingford House to plead for 'relief in her necessities', but Buckingham denied her everything, told her to leave and when she attempted to reason with him, she was 'most barbarously carryed by force into the street and there left void of all reliefe'.

She consulted her lawyer, Mr. Elrich, and on his advice she wrote an appealing letter, hoping to elicit some sympathy. 'For your honour and conscience sake, take some course to give me satisfaction, to tye my tongue from crying to God and to the world for vengeance for the unworthy dealing I have received, lest I begg my bread in the street to all your dishonours.'

When she got no reply to this letter, she wrote again, this time pleading at least for the return of her husband. 'Though you can judge, my Lord, what pleasure there is in the conversation of a man in the distemper you see your brother in, yet the duty I owe to a husband and the affection I bear him (which sicknesse shall not diminish) makes me much desire to be with him to add what comfort I can to his afflicted mind since his only desire is my company, which if it please you I shall with a very good will satisfie him in, though I think every wife would not. But if you so far dispense with the laws of God to keep me from my husband, yet aggravate it not by restraining me from his means and all other contentments; but which I think is rather the part of a Christian you specially ought much rather study comforts for me than to add ills to ill. For if you please but to consider not only the lamentable state I am in, deprived of all comforts of a husband and having no means to live, besides falling from the hope my fortune then did promise me, for you know very well that I came no beggar to you, though I am likely to be so turned off ...'

Frances was desperate, but Buckingham was not to be moved. During all this time she had no option but to seek shelter in Hatton House. It was almost unendurable for her to find herself beholden to the person who had betrayed her into this miserable marriage.

Finally Lady Hatton arrived back from Corfe, went straight to the King and implored justice from him. James pointed out to Buckingham that as he was enjoying £30,000 of his sister-in-law's money, he might allow her some small sum to save her from destitution. In due course, Frances received an allowance of £600 a year and her apartments in Denmark House, but only on condition that she signed a pledge to keep away from her husband – and to this she reluctantly had to agree. However, whenever John escaped or recovered sufficiently, he hurried to her side and his love for her remained deep and unquestioning and he once remarked that although her dowry was welcome, 'I would have taken her in her shift.'

Frances began to find life more tolerable. Being of a naturally merry disposition and a favourite with everyone, excepting her mother-in-law, she now had lodgings in Denmark House and could join in all the festivities, dinners, masques and river pageants with her many friends, and she was no longer required to be in the constant company of her husband and his eccentricities.

Her allowance, although frugal, saved her from real want, but perhaps best of all, a matter of greater importance distracted Buckingham from the persecution of his sister-in-law. Buckingham had fallen deeply in love with Lady Katherine Manners, the only daughter of the Duke of Rutland. Unfortunately, the family was one of the leading Catholic families in the country. The Catholic religion was forbidden and there were stringent penalties against its practice, and for the King's favourite to marry someone of that faith would only increase his unpopularity in the country, so for a time James forbade Buckingham to marry her.

Nevertheless Buckingham pursued his courtship resolutely and one day his mother invited Katherine Manners to spend the day with her. Towards evening the Countess fell ill and insisted the girl stay with her. When Katherine returned home next day, her father refused her entrance, believing that her honour had been besmirched. Despite all explanation, he turned her out, so with little alternative she took refuge in the Buckingham household and a marriage took place quickly, quietly, privately and illegally.

Katherine adored her handsome husband and their marriage was a very happy one. Subsequently she took instruction and joined the Church of England, but it was an anxious period for everybody. However, James, despite his infatuation with Buckingham, in no wise resented the marriage and accepted Katherine as a daughter, although he frequently referred to her as 'that puir fool Kate'. He was delighted when the following year she became pregnant.

Throughout this time Frances was left in peace and happily joined in the round of court activities, forever on the move, usually in Whitehall from October until New Year, when James would joyfully go to Newmarket or Royston to indulge in his favourite pastime of hunting. There was much unspoken criticism of him for neglecting kingly business for his own enjoyment, but he maintained that hunting was essential to his health. 'He findes such felicitie,' writes one of the courtiers, 'in that hunting life that He hath written to the consaile that yt is the only meanes to maintain His health (which being the health and welfare of us all) He desires them to foresee that He be not interrupted nor troubled with too much business.' James disliked ceremonies and hated being viewed by the general public, and when reminded that his people delighted to see him, he replied with his usual coarseness, 'God's wounds, I'll pull down my breeches and they shall also see my arse.'

His courtiers found hunting far less pleasurable. It meant forsaking the comfort of Whitehall for crowded expensive lodgings elsewhere. They would be in the saddle by eight in the morning and hunt till four, after which there might be a five-mile ride home.

Ladies attended when deer were driven past screened ambushes and both men and women shot with the crossbow, but once the men were mounted, the ladies did not accompany them. They also were inclined to find these weeks of hunting tedious, but no-one dared forsake the royal person for fear of missing opportunities or losing favour. The possibilities were enormous and uncertain. For the fortunate few who happened to be in the right place at the right time, there were unbelievable favours to be got – titles, ecclesiastical benefits, estates of persons attainted, wardships, appointments, monopolies or royal benevolence. In James' corrupt court all these were saleable, inheritable and transferable.

Farmers were equally unhappy about hunting. Their land and crops were damaged, they received no benefit, and their cry was, 'Let him hear, good God, the sounds and cries of men as well as hounds', but James loved his hunting and savagely enforced the laws against poachers.

It was his strange distasteful custom when a stag was killed to plunge his legs into the animal's bowels, for he fully believed that it would ward off sicknesses of all kinds.

In 1623 Frances felt almost light-hearted when her persecutor, Buckingham, left the country. In a madcap scheme Prince Charles, accompanied by Buckingham, decided to gallop across France incognito to woo the Infanta of Spain. At first James was desperate at the idea of parting with Buckingham – rather than his own son – and wrote to him, 'My own sweet and dear child, I am now so miserable a coward as I do nothing but weep and mourn for I protest to God that I rode out this afternoon a great way in the park without speaking to anybody and the tears running down my cheeks. Alas, what shall I do at our parting?'

Despite the royal grief, the pair set off and nearly caused a diplomatic incident by passing through France without requesting passage from the French King, but presently James cheered up sufficiently to write to them, 'My sweet boys and dear venturous knights, worthy to be put into a new romanso.' In order to add to the dignity of their mission, he sent papers creating Buckingham a Duke, the first to be created outside the royal family since before the days of Queen Elizabeth. By this time, Prince Charles had lost any previous jealousy and had become as devoted to

Buckingham as his father; he had entirely succumbed to the favourite's extraordinary ability to charm.

Sadly, the Spanish enterprise was a fiasco. They went in disguise, but their identity was revealed immediately. They offended everyone in that dignified court with their foolish pranks and childish behaviour, and Buckingham so far forgot himself as to make advances to the Queen, probably certain that no-one could resist him. The Spanish nobility were so scandalized that they declared that they would rather see the Infanta enter a convent than go to the English court.

The Queen 'however' was gracious to Charles and conversed with him while the Ambassdor, the Earl of Bristol, knelt before them acting as an interpreter. She allowed him to lead her to open the dancing at a magnificent ball in their honour. And clad in black velvet and mounted on a fine horse, Charles rode into the ring at the Plaza Mayor before a bull fight.

The real purpose of their visit was to enlist Spain's help for James' daughter, Elizabeth, the Protestant Queen of Bohemia, and to cement this with the engagement of Prince Charles to the Infanta. They failed in both objectives. They were entertained royally for six months, but they gained neither military help nor bride and finally they were called home by James. They got a tumultuous reception from the English populace when they landed, everyone being delighted that they had returned without a Catholic Princess.

Frances was dining with other friends in a merry throng when Prince Charles and Buckingham arrived back and they all rose in greeting. The Prince acknowledged their applause and stopped to greet them, but the newly appointed Duke strode past them arrogantly and went straight to the King's apartments with an air of discontent. It appeared that Buckingham was deeply offended by the cool reception that they had received in Spain and he chafed at their lack of diplomatic success. To crown his discontent, later that evening he heard, with anger and disbelief, a rumour that Frances was pregnant.

So far Katherine had borne him two children, both daughters, and one had died in infancy. By the letters patent creating him a duke, the title, should he die without a male heir, would pass to his brother John and his heirs. The idea that the title might pass to a bastard, fathered he believed by Sir Robert Howard, was intolerable, and his dislike of his sister-in-law turned truly venomous as he plotted his revenge.

Buckingham's Anger

A few weeks after the travellers' return, Frances had retired early to her rooms and was already in bed when she heard a hubbub of laughing voices drawing ever nearer her apartment and the sound of footsteps on her stairway. She wondered whether to get up to investigate, but then her door burst open and in strode Buckingham with his mother and an elderly woman who was dressed in sombre modest clothing quite unlike that of the rest of the laughing prurient party who crowded in. Buckingham announced that they had come to ascertain whether she was truly pregnant.

Frances shrank back in horror, but before she could protest, the bedclothes were pulled roughly away, leaving her exposed to all their eager eyes. Despite her cries, she was held down by Edward Villiers, George's half brother, whilst the elderly woman, who turned out to be a midwife, was ordered to carry out an intimate examination. It was hardly necessary, for it was clear to all who saw her swollen belly that she was indeed heavily with child, but before them all it proceeded. Then they all withdraw with hoots of cruel laughter.

Frances lay there, sick with humiliation and anger, mortified that anyone should expose her so publicly. She had been roughly handled, not seriously hurt, but she determined there and then that she would have to hide if she and the baby were to survive and she dared remain no longer in Denmark House.

The very next day she began her search, and before the week was out she had found and moved into lodgings with a Mrs. Manning of White Cross Street, in a small inconspicuous house where she would be unlikely to be traced. She took only one personal maid and very few possessions and she settled down for the remaining weeks of her pregnancy. She barely went out of the house for fear of being seen, although it was unpleasant to be so confined after the large and lofty rooms to which she was accustomed.

She told no-one of her whereabouts, ever fearful of Buckingham's spies. She sewed a little and read, but she found it difficult to concentrate on anything in her distress, as her body changed and became uncomfortable, making her movements awkward, and the nights afforded her only fitful sleep. She wondered endlessly about her future and that of her child, for she had no resources now that Buckingham had taken everything and he would surely stop her allowance. She devoutly hoped that the child might be a girl which would pose no threat as heir to the dukedom.

Once or twice, greatly daring, she put on a dark cloak and covered her head and made the short journey to the Church of St. Giles in Cripplegate, where she knelt in prayer before the statue of the Virgin Mary and begged her for help and for strength in the coming days.

On 16th October her maid discovered her at the side of the bed, holding her sides in pain. The girl ran to Mrs. Manning who went quickly to summon the midwife and Frances began to feel pain such as she had never believed possible. The day went on and she turned, groaning, from side to side. Mrs. Manning wanted to call her mother, but Frances, her face damp with sweat, shook her head. The midwife gave her a soothing posset and assured her that it was all quite normal and that her sufferings were no worse than that of many others. Her maid wiped her face with cooling cloths and the day faded into an anguished night.

At last, just as dawn was breaking, the child was born and there came the welcome sound of a baby's cry. 'Is it a girl?' Frances whispered, almost too exhausted and weak to speak. 'No, no, you are fortunate, my Lady, you have a beautiful son.' Tears ran down Frances' cheeks and those present all believed that they were tears of joy.

Her whereabouts were disclosed when the child was christened. Although this took place privately in the garden of White Cross Street, a notice appeared in the Church of St. Giles. The baby was baptized Robert Wright and the name of the father was given as John Wright of Bishopsthorpe.

Once the baby was born and the secret was out, Frances realised that she could not hide for ever and that it was probably safer to return to Denmark House where there would always be people about to assist her. She hired a nurse, Mistress Wells, the daughter of a well-known barber with premises in the Strand, and they returned to her previous apartments. Robert was often in attendance. Her friends came to visit her, as well as her mother, who admired her new grandson, but asked no questions about the presumed father.

If she had imagined that she would be allowed to live in peace, she was sadly mistaken, for Buckingham was so incensed that he gave the King no peace until he agreed that Frances and Robert Howard be brought before the courts and accused of adultery. The King's health was failing and he was in a pitiable physical condition, but Buckingham gave him no respite and pursued the matter remorselessly. He wrote angrily to the Lord Chancellor, 'I understand that you are not yet resolved to commit my sister Purbeck, who if she be at liberty, will be still plotting and devising with her ill counsellors to cover and conceal the truth and foulness of her crime, and my brother will be every day running to her and give her occasion to work on him by the subtlety of her discourse.'

James was too weak and ill to protest, so he agreed that the trial should proceed, and in his determination to destroy Frances, Buckingham wrote to the Attorney General, 'We desire you principally to aggravate her crime, so that by my humble and your kind like favour, the lady may yet be kept in prison'.

Frances was in no way dismayed and resolutely denied all the accusations made against her. She was taken for a preliminary hearing before the Lord Chief Justice, the Attorney General, the Solicitor General and others, all of whom were only too anxious to please Buckingham. It was a formidable array, as they sat in their robes in a semi-circle, whilst Frances stood before them, a slight but upright figure who declared their accusations outrageous. Privately she was heard to remark that she wondered what those old cuckolds had to say to her and they in turn found her an unsatisfactory witness. Robert Howard kept silence, pleading privilege as a Member of Parliament, so the examiners finally reported, 'We cannot gain any express confession from the parties or testimony that can prove them guilty.'

Frances and Robert believed that they had heard the last

of the affair but this was far from so, and at Buckingham's insistence the two were committed for trial at the Court of High Commission, the highest ecclesiastical court in the land, the very court denounced by Frances' father. Lady Hatton was so concerned that she forgot all her dislike of him and went to ask her husband for his help, but he had made peace with Buckingham for the time being and had no sympathy with his daughter's foolish conduct, so he declined to take any part in the matter.

As the day drew near for her appearance at the court hearing, Frances began to feel unwell, and although friends assured her that it was only the anxiety over her coming ordeal that was bothering her, she grew steadily worse. Her head throbbed and she felt burning hot and icy cold by turns and every limb ached unbearably. She knew that she could not stand up in court and she sent word that she was not fit to stand trial, but Buckingham believed that she was feigning illness and ordered the trial to continue. Just two days before she was due to appear, she arose after a sleepless night to find that she was covered in pustules, a victim of the dreaded illness, smallpox.

There was no question of her leaving her bed, she was far too ill to attend court, and no-one wanted to catch that highly infectious and dreaded disease. For some days her life was in danger. As soon as John heard of her illness, he managed to escape and go to her and refused to leave her bedside until she recovered. A fire was kept burning in her room night and day, the curtains were tightly drawn, sweet herbs were strewn on the floor and fresh garlands were hung around the walls each morning. The leading physician Dr. Theodore Mayerns was called, but there was very little treatment for smallpox; sponges soaked in vinegar soothed her fevered body as she lay half conscious, too ill even to worry what the pox might do to her beauty.

Her condition should have been enough to move the hardest heart, but not Buckingham's; she was still pale and weak, convalescing, and not able to walk with ease when he ordered the Lord Chief Justice to continue the case, and in order to complete her ruin he decided to bring an additional charge of witchcraft. Remembering her visit to Dr. Lambe, he wrote to the Attorney General and suggested that Lambe and his assistant, Frodsham, should give evidence that Frances had paid them to bewitch him and his brother. He wrote sinisterly to Lord Coventry, the Attorney General, 'If Frodsham and Lambe can feele or be brought to fear their punishment, I believe that they will unfolde much more than they have yet.'

By coincidence, Sir Edward Coke unwittingly helped Frances in that he had recently changed the law. Previously, prisoners who refused to speak could be 'pressed', which entailed pressing them with ever heavier weights until they spoke or died. Sir Edward held that the accused had the right to keep silence, and it so happened that his daughter was one of the first to avail themselves of this change in the law. Robert also kept silence, but it was generally assumed that they would be found guilty as a favour to Buckingham. There was an anxious time whilst the judges deliberated, and in a last attempt to help, Robert's mother Lady Suffolk declared that 'her son was insufficient'.

Suddenly the silence in the court was broken by noise and confusion at the back. Heads turned and Frances too looked round and gazed in disbelief, for there in the doorway was John, pale and dishevelled as he edged forward towards the judges. Frances looked at the pathetic shambling figure of her husband and wondered whatever he was about to do. Judges and public alike gazed as he stood and looked around until he saw Frances, smiled and declared loudly that the child was his.

There was a gasp and then a spontaneous outburst of applause before the officials called sternly for silence. The judges were nonplussed, but after admitting that there was some slight but unproven suggestion of witchcraft, they quickly decided that they had now no option but to acquit because, as the law stood, legitimacy was presumed unless it could be proved that access was impossible or the husband was impotent.

Immediately after the case, the Attorney General wrote to Buckingham apologetically, explaining why they had been unable to make the accused speak, which was entirely due to the change which Sir Edward had brought about in the law. 'Sir Edward Coke (preseeing out of a prophetical) how near it might concern a grandchild of his some day, hath expunged the clause and left us nothing but the rusty Sword, Excommunication, to vindicate the authority of the Church.'

Frances and Robert rejoiced and London rejoiced and laughed with them over their victory, and there was enormous delight at Buckingham's discomfiture. He did not attempt to conceal his anger. He was not used to being thwarted and before long Frances realized that her triumph was only temporary.

For a while, however, she was quite forgotten because, just a few days after her acquittal, King James died and was succeeded by his son, Charles. Buckingham was busy with the funeral and, more importantly, with preparations for the coming coronation.

The plague was very bad that year and to escape it, as well as to seek peace after all the anxiety of her trial, Frances took her child and her household down to Stepney. This was quite rural and a welcome change from the crowded conditions at Whitehall. Now that her income was smaller, Frances had had to reduce the number of servants that she employed. Two of her former footmen, Thomas Worley and Daniel Dickinson, were now unemployed and they were approached by an agent, on behalf of Buckingham, with the suggestion that they should murder Frances and her son. For this task they were offered £50 apiece and they were to escape to France after the crime had been successfully carried out. They would be given a free pardon to return at the time of King Charles' coronation.

Thomas accordingly went to the father of Mistress Wells, the child Robert's nurse, and casually asked about his daughter's whereabouts. This was given without any demur, but when Thomas started to ask detailed questions about the household, Mr. Wells grew suspicious. He discussed the matter with his wife and the upshot was that they contacted Mr. Elrich, Frances' excellent lawyer, who hastened down to Stepney, possibly only just in time.

Thomas Worley and his accomplice had already got into the house and were standing, sword in hand, in the hall. Frances' gentlewomen caught sight of them and fled in terror, reporting the presence of alarming-looking strangers holding naked swords. Seizing the child from his cot, the women bolted the doors of the bedroom, drew the furniture across the door and stood with beating hearts awaiting their fate. With admirable courage, Mr. Elrich, having just arrived, accosted the two men and eventually frightened them sufficiently to cause both scoundrels to disappear rapidly.

It was an oddly botched, clumsy attempt on their lives.

However, Frances was distraught and ordered that every door and window should be bolted and barred, and the child was never allowed to leave the house. She had always feared her arrogant brother-in-law, but it had never occurred to her that he would actually hire assassins to kill her and her baby. She had fervently hoped that under King Charles Buckingham's influence might not be so powerful, but in fact this extraordinary man exercised even more influence over Charles than he ever had over James.

The game of cat and mouse continued, but mercifully all persecution ceased when in November that year the Duchess of Buckingham gave birth to a son. He was christened Charles and there was enormous rejoicing and great celebration, and in their joy Frances was momentarily forgotten, so she too had a wonderful Christmas and New Year, with presents and feasting and many a banquet with Sir Robert as usual as her escort.

Alas, her jubilation was short lived, for in the following April she learnt with dismay that Buckingham's little son, Charles, was ill. Rumour followed rumour, sometimes the child was making a recovery and sometimes he had a relapse, but nobody wished more fervently for his health than Frances. Within a few weeks the child died and before they had even ceased their anguished mourning, and perhaps to assuage their grief, Buckingham ordered a new trial in order 'to clarify the legitimacy of the boy Robert Wright' and Frances knew in her heart that even John's intervention might not save her this time.

It was a lonely time for her, since she was denied access to her husband, her father had declined to help her and she was too proud to seek her mother's aid. She was aware that Buckingham would be careful to choose his judges and select only those who owed their promotion to him or those who were seeking his favour. She could not ask for Robert's help because, by so doing, she would risk incriminating both him and herself. She had neither the funds nor the inclination to flee the country, for her life and her heart were firmly planted in the court and she neither knew nor desired any other way of life.

A Sentence is Pronounced

Frances dressed very carefully that November morning. With foreboding, she looked out of the window at a dank autumn scene as the wind swirled leaves helter skelter along the muddy roadways and only those on urgent business were about. She chose a green grogram gown which set off her fair curls, her collar was spotlessly white and freshly laundered, but she fidgeted as her maid arranged her hair in ringlets and she shivered involuntarily and pulled her cloak tightly around her as she entered her coach.

The Court of High Commission sat at Lambeth Palace, so she was rowed across the misty Thames. Despite the fact that it was nearing midday, it was gloomy and candles were already alight so that papers might be read more easily. The case had aroused much interest and there was a crowd of spectators. Frances hesitated a moment as she entered the lofty panelled room flanked by two stalwart guards, and she looked quickly and apprehensively at her judges. She then advanced with a composure which belied her inner feelings. The panel included Sir Thomas Coventry, Keeper of the Great Seal, the Earl of Manchester, Lord President of the Council, the Earl of Pembroke, Lord Steward, the Earl of Montgomery, Lord Chamberlain, and the Bishops of London, Durham, Norwich, Rochester and Laud (soon to become Archbishop of Canterbury).They were a truly imposing group, all too many owing their positions to Buckingham's patronage.

Frances tried hard to concentrate as they questioned her at length and in great depth, and everyone agreed that she answered 'very wittily'. Not for nothing was her father the most astute lawyer in the Kingdom. When they asked why she had called her child Robert Wright, the disgraceful scene in her bedroom was graphically described. 'Endeavouring to ruin her in honour and fortune, the Countess of Buckingham with many others in a riotous manner entered her room and barbarously haled her out of bed. Sir Edward Villiers, being of the company, held her by force upon pretence that midwives or others should examine her. This enforced her to withdraw herself to a private place unknown to her adversaries and to take upon her a feigned name both for herself and the son born of her body and to pretend herself to have been the wife of John Wright, thereby to conceal both herself and the child from the rage and fury which she had just cause, upon her former barbarous usage, to fear and suspect.'

She described how she had concealed herself until the birth and how she had feared for her life at the hands of her footmen and how her cruel brother-in-law had taken all her goods and means of livelihood.

As she finished this account of her humiliation, there was a loud murmur of sympathy from the listening public, and although it was quickly hushed by the officials, general sympathy was clearly strongly with Frances. This vexed the prosecution and one of the Bishop's servants was punished when he declared loudly and publicly that Lady Purbeck was being hardly dealt with.

She rejected contemptuously the allegation that Robert had entered her bedroom through the roof, saying that this was mere discontented servants' gossiping. Sir Robert, as before, kept silence, pleading his right as Member of Parliament, and the trial dragged on through the afternoon. Finally, at the end of her questioning, Frances asked that her husband be called upon to give evidence on her behalf. There was a long silence, then the Countess of Buckingham replied that regrettably her son was too sick in mind and body to attend court or speak reliably, adding waspishly that it must be presumed that his wife's conduct had contributed to his plight. Frances' heart sank, since she had named her special oppressors, Lady Buckingham and the hateful Sir

Edward Villiers, and she knew that to obtain her conviction they would use all means to stop John testifying, for none of the Buckingham family wanted a repetition of the last occasion when John's evidence had saved her and made a laughing stock of them.

Frances remained proud and silent whilst her judges considered their verdict, although with Buckingham's pervasive influence the result was almost a foregone conclusion. After an indecently short interval, both parties were declared guilty.

Sir Robert Howard was sentenced to public excommunication at St. Paul's for his refusal to speak, committed to prison and fined for adultery. For Frances the sentence was even more savage. She also was convicted of adultery, committed to prison and fined, but she was sentenced to penance, which meant walking barefoot, clad only in a white shift with a lighted candle in her hand, from St. Paul's to the Savoy Chapel. She gave an involuntary cry, paled and swayed on her feet as the humiliating sentence was read out. In order to make her misery complete, the sentence was postponed until the next public holiday, when all of London's apprentices would be free to taunt, throw rotten eggs and vegetables and generally torment their victim. To do this to a high-born lady would give them especial delight and Frances had seen for herself how hideously penitents could be wounded. She could not hide her anguish as she was led away by guards to the Gate House to await her horrible punishment.

Mercifully for her, she lived in such a corrupt age that money and influence could achieve almost anything, and when the time for her penance came, Frances had vanished. Her gaoler was accused, demoted and punished, but he professed absolute ignorance, and how her remarkable escape was managed remained for ever a secret. Robert was in prison, her father had refused to help, so it must be assumed that Lady Hatton had a hand in it. Her disappearance mystified everybody and all kinds of rumours circulated around her – that she had been murdered in prison or had fled the country, but nobody knew where she was or how her escape had been manoeuvred.

Buckingham and his family were incensed that this wretched girl had made fools of them once again and he determined to find her and to ensure that justice be done and the penance carried out. He sent out innumerable spies and finally discovered that Frances and the child had taken refuge in a small house standing within the Savoy Embassy grounds where diplomatic immunity made it impossible for her to be arrested.

Buckingham immediately put a guard on the front door which gave onto the street, but he could not force an entrance because the house was in Savoy grounds. He could not even put a guard on the back door because that was in the Savoy garden. He demanded access but to no avail. This was the third time that Frances had outwitted him and he was determined on revenge, and since his favourite was displeased, the King was angry and affronted also when the guards were refused entry.

He threatened to have the Ambassador recalled and to break off diplomatic relations with Savoy. To emphasize his vexation, he denied the Ambassador audience at court, a mark of highest displeasure. It was a predicament for all, especially for the Ambassador, because if he refused the King's request, he risked his own career and feared that the state of Savoy might lose the friendship of a rich and powerful nation. On the other hand, he had followed the case and found Frances' plight infinitely moving and he hesitated to turn away a beautiful young woman and her baby, especially as all London was on her side, so he temporised in true diplomatic fashion.

Frances was too terrified to be jubilant at her escape. Her life seemed to be repeating itself and she kept remembering her horrible experience when she and her mother had taken shelter at Oatlands and the outcome had been her disastrous marriage. Eight years of marriage had brought her no happiness and almost continual fear. She had never feared her strange and strangely loving husband, however oddly he behaved, but the Villiers family had threatened her, taken all her money, and tried to murder her and her child and she could see no escape from her persecution.

The Ambassador reluctantly finally agreed to allow one guard, and one guard only, into the Savoy grounds to watch over the back door, and to this compromise the King gave a grudging assent. Everybody settled down to wait out the apparent stalemate, but a daring plan was afoot.

One morning a coach and six drew up outside the back door and a slim, cloaked and hooded figure carrying a bundle stepped out, looked anxiously right and left and quickly entered the coach, which set off at a gallop. The guard shouted a loud halloo to his fellows and within minutes all were mounted and in pursuit, but the coach was going at a cracking pace along the Strand and soon passed out of sight; bystanders were not slow to point out the direction it had taken and the men on horseback were quicker than any coach. Within a mile they overtook it and brought it to a halt and down stepped a young page who professed himself astonished at being held up and showed that he was merely carrying a bundle of washing in his arms.

Meanwhile, at the Embassy not a second was wasted. The moment the guards had left, Mistress Wells, with the child in her arms, hurried out to a waiting conveyance and left swiftly. Then Frances mounted behind a young man on a sturdy horse and they trotted off, travelling as fast as they dared without attracting overmuch attention to themselves. Their first anxiety was to get out of the neighbourhood before the alarm was raised, and to their relief they passed safely beyond Tyburn unchallenged, then turned west to Islington where they were soon in open fields.

There had been no time for speech or explanation. Frances had only received a message that very morning telling her to be ready, that the child would go to her mother at Corfe and that Robert had sent his steward to fetch her and take her safely to his home in Clun where they would meet as soon as he was released from prison. It was not felt possible for a young child to undertake so hazardous a journey.

Frances was gripped with fear, in panic lest she should yet again feel the guards' arms on her, leading her back to prison. She froze and tried not to look around whenever she heard horses behind her, and her heart was beating wildly as she clutched her guide tightly for fear of falling. It was February weather at its worst. Sleety rain was blown into their faces by the icy wind and the roads were a morass of mud. The horse slipped and slithered, sometimes almost up to its belly in cart tracks full of water. There were few travellers about and only once did they see fit to take refuge in a nearby wood when they heard a great tumult far behind them, but no-one looked their way and the troop passed by, shouting and flogging their mounts. Daylight started to fade and at Hampstead they changed their horse, but they still pressed on, almost as fearful now of footpads or bands of robbers as they were of pursuit.

Frances was exhausted and wet through with the rain and the driving wind and felt that she could go no further. 'Where do we stay to-night?' she asked forlornly. Her escort, she learnt, was called Tom, 'Tom Feather, my Lady', and he told her that he had done the journey before and that he had friends in quiet inns where they could pass the night in safety.

She looked at him and felt a sense of security. He was small and stocky with a mop of red hair and a ruddy beard and, she judged, in his late thirties; he looked immensely strong and she felt that she could believe him when he assured her that he would bring her to safety. But now he had time to look at her, and he excused himself when he saw how tired, cold and wet she looked, saying only that his master had urged him to spare no time in bringing her out of London. He had brought her a cloak, apologizing that it was not fit for a lady, but it was thicker and warmer and would keep out the rain better than her own light and delicate one and she accepted it gratefully.

They lay that night in Watford, Tom explaining that they were travelling further north to avoid Stoke Poges where they might be sought, but they rested for only a few hours, and before it was fully daylight they set off again. The weather in the morning was kinder, and she felt a little less anxious and every now and then just a trace of satisfaction that once more she had eluded the worst designs of her cruel brother-in-law.

'Where do we lie to-night, Tom?' she enquired. 'Thame, my Lady', he replied. 'We dare not risk Oxford – we might be questioned there or you might be recognized. I'll not feel easy until we see Ludlow Castle.'

Safety and Boredom

It was a gruelling undertaking. Their journey was slow since they dared not enter large towns or cross rivers on major bridges, but day by day they travelled ever further from danger, although the roads grew muddier and the inns were rougher. From Thame they made their way to Moreton-in-Marsh, which lived up to its name.

Several times they had to turn back from low-lying land, too deep in mud, and more than once they looked at the swirling brown water where a ford was indicated and Tom shook his head and dared not risk their getting swept away or sucked down into the boggy wastes. This meant they often had to make long detours.

It was eight days before they reached Leominster and late the following afternoon the proud outline of Ludlow rose against the evening skyline. Ludlow was the seat of the Lord of the Marches and very much a stronghold of authority. 'A messenger could have arrived here before us and we will take no chances. We'll be at Bromfield to-night and safe with friends,' declared Tom. Frances sensed the relief in voice as he neared his familiar country and the burden of his mission lessened. In her own deep fear she had scarcely thought of the anxieties that he must have felt and with remorse she expressed her thanks for all his care.

She looked up at the town silhouetted against the dim moonlit wintry sky and she sighed a little. How far she felt from London and Whitehall and her many friends and she wondered wistfully when or if ever she would return, and what could possibly lie ahead for her. For the moment there was trouble enough without worrying about the future, for it had started to snow and flake on flake fluttered across her eyes, mesmerising her, and soon the ground turned white. The going became so treacherous with holes camouflaged by snow that Tom dismounted and led the horse and they continued at a snail's pace, cold and tired, but now safe from any pursuers.

At last, towards dusk the following day they reached Clun and crossed the ancient bridge. It had been snowing gently all day and Frances felt unutterably weary as she glanced up at the bleak outline of the old castle which looked ominously dark and ruined.

'Do we go to the Castle, Tom?' she asked apprehensively.

'Oh no, my Lady, that has been in ruins many a long day. We are bound for the Hall of the Forest ten miles up the valley.'

'Ten more miles,' she murmured and there was no mistaking the fatigue and despair in her voice.

'My Lady, will you lie tonight here in Clun? The Sun Inn is close by in the main street. It is a good inn and I know the landlord. You will be safe here and I will go to the Hall of the Forest and tell them of your coming. They will make everything ready and I will fetch you in the morning when you are rested.'

Frances nodded in gratitude. She was so frozen and exhausted that she could hardly walk into the parlour. She stumbled thankfully towards a large log fire to thaw her stiff and icy hands and feet, whilst Tom spoke to the landlord. She stood close to the welcome warmth. She ate sparingly, and then with relief she sank into a feather bed, wonderfully heated by a warming pan. 'I am free, I am safe,' she kept thinking until sleep shut out the cold, the snow and the uncertainty.

It was still early when Frances was awoken by the sounds of horses and men shouting beneath her window. All her fears returned as she recalled with horror how she had been assaulted once before as she lay in bed. She rose and dressed hurriedly. She was now used to dressing herself, for in prison it was something she had perforce had to learn. Once clothed, she pulled the old worsted cloak around her and peered through the curtains and almost cried with relief as she saw, not guards or soldiers, but farmers herding their cattle into the yard behind the inn. Bidding was taking place, money changing hands and new owners driving their beasts away.

Frances left the inn unobserved and made her way to the little Church of St. George, built with walls as stout as any fortress. There she entered and knelt and looked up at the angels that held up the roof and thought with deep gratitude of the many people who had helped her to escape, but above all she prayed for her two Roberts, pleading that her son might have reached safety at Purbeck Castle, that her beloved Robert be let out of prison and that they might soon all be reunited. It was quiet as she sat for a few moments and the thick walls kept the outside world away, and it was with a more peaceful mind that she returned to the bustle of the Sun Inn where Tom awaited her.

The ground was still snow covered and the going was slushy, but a wintry sun shone through the dark pine trees as they made their way up the narrow valley where they met neither man nor beast during their ride. Finally they came to a little clearing and turned downhill towards a substantial farmhouse, set in a small oasis in the forest. It was surrounded on every side by tall trees, and through their swaying branches high above them was a glimpse of snowy hilltops. On this dreary February morning it looked lonely and desolate.

As they approached the door, an elderly man and his grey-haired wife came out to meet them. 'Barra dach,' they said in unison and the man bowed and his wife bobbed a curtsey. As Tom helped Frances down, the couple spoke a torrent of Welsh and Tom explained. 'They speak no English, but they are welcoming you to the Hall of the Forest.'

Frances had a moment of panic and looked regretfully after Tom as he saluted her and remounted and she watched him disappearing into the trees. She took a deep breath and turned to enter her new home.

At least I am in safety, she kept telling herself. She was ushered into a flagstoned hall and thence into a parlour where a fire was burning brightly and here the old woman left her and retired, closing the door behind her. She crossed to the window and watched some hens scratching, and ducks and geese swimming on a small pond in the middle of the courtyard, and she could hear cattle in the distance. All around the dark trees were blowing in the wind and the hills above looked infinitely menacing. She shivered and turned back to the warmth of the grate.

She wondered how she could make her wishes known. She longed for a change of clothing since she had fled with nothing except what she was wearing and her dress was now sadly torn, damp and mud stained. Presently the old woman returned, bearing bread and meat and beer which she put on the table and beckoned to Frances to come and eat. 'Gwyneth' she said and pointed to herself. Frances repeated it once or twice until she got a nod of approval and then she pointed to her own dress and held up the muddy hem. Gwyneth murmured a few words and went away, leaving Frances wondering how much she had understood, but that very afternoon a woman appeared and brought some material for her approval. It was coarsely woven homespun, quite different from anything that Frances had ever worn before, but much better than nothing, and two dresses appeared remarkably quickly. She sighed a little as she remembered her own store of garments of quilted satin, lace and brocade, ornamented with precious stones and trimmed with costly lace, dresses that she had enjoyed wearing and the joyous occasions when she had worn them. She wondered whether she would ever again return to the court and all her friends.

The days seemed long and tedious and the weather was so atrocious that she dared not venture out. Gwyneth and Huw were kind and served her diligently and brought her homely well-cooked meals, but she found it difficult to learn enough Welsh to have a conversation. She searched the house, but there were no books, not even a Bible or a pamphlet, and then she discovered that neither Gwyneth nor her husband could read.

At last she found a spinning wheel in the attic, and with sign language and Gwyneth's help, she got a supply of wool. How she longed to have someone to talk to and someone to laugh with her and at her, as her unaccustomed fingers tangled and broke the yarn. Her results were not impressive, but Gwyneth did not laugh, only gently corrected her poor efforts as she redoubled her attempts. But her thoughts were elsewhere. What she urgently wanted was news of the people and the world she knew. Was she still being sought, was her child safe, was Robert released and why did he not come as he had promised?

One day there was a sudden commotion and Gwyneth hurried in to her and beckoned her outside. Tom had saddled a pony and was waiting for her. He told her that there were soldiers in Clun and nobody yet knew the purpose of their visit, so he wished to take her away to safety in the hills in case they were seeking her. He walked beside her pony and led her along a rough path, always upwards until they reached a little bothy used by shepherds during lambing. He begged her to stay there until his return and assured her that no-one would ever find her there, then he hurried away to reconnoitre.

It was the utter silence that oppressed her, a silence more profound than she had ever known before, and she looked over the beautiful countryside and unashamedly wept for London, for the court, for companionship, for someone to talk to, for a word in English, for bustle and gaiety and friends. She was cold and hungry before Tom returned and she learnt with relief that it was a false alarm. The soldiers were on a tour of the district to collect all prisoners from jail to take them to the assizes in Ludlow. He apologized to her for the anxiety he had caused her, but explained that he would always be at her side if strangers were about and she could feel perfectly secure that no-one would ever approach the Hall of the Forest without his knowing. Frances thanked him warmly for his kindness, but the episode had unsettled her, and she alternated between gratitude for her escape and frustration at the tedium of her life here alone. She had now been at Clun for many weeks, and with no word from the outer world, she felt betrayed and forgotten.

It was late August when a peddler appeared. He was a regular traveller round the villages and farms where he sold ribbons and thread, pins and needles, lace and many another little trifles. He was always welcome and found some custom, but he was also especially welcome because of the news he brought of the world outside. He was in the kitchen when Gwyneth knocked on the parlour door and beckoned excitedly. Frances duly followed her, and found the peddler unpacking his wares on the kitchen table and to her delight he spoke English, the first time she had heard English spoken in that house, but the news that he brought was so sensational that she made him repeat it several times to make certain that she had understood correctly.

The great Duke of Buckingham, he assured her, was dead, murdered by a man called Fulton in Portsmouth, and the whole of England was rejoicing. Frances was speechless – she could feel no sorrow, for he had persecuted her too cruelly, indeed she was filled with hope and wonder, for this would surely mean that she could now return to London and to her previous life.

After the peddler had gone, she walked up the hill behind the farm, a walk that she had become accustomed to take during the long summer evenings, and she looked around her. Heather on the hills glowed in splendour and she could hear a skylark singing, but as she sat on the short turf she wondered whether her crippled life would ever mend, for even if she returned to London, she had pledged never to approach her husband again, and yet as she was not a widow, where and how was she to live. If only, she thought once again, her mother had never agreed to that marriage or her father had not been so anxious to return to favour. She forgot the beauty of the evening and returned to the farmhouse disconsolate and thoughtful.

Not many days later Robert appeared, dusty and exhausted by his swift ride from London. Gwyneth and Huw fussed round him with obvious affection and it was only after he had eaten and drunk and changed his travel worn clothes that Frances and he were able to talk together privately.

He gave her the first important news – that her little son was safely living at Corfe with his nurse, Mistress Wells, and as he kissed her he smiled at her homespun appearance, so different from the last time they had met, but he assured her when she blushed and looked down at her peasant dress apologetically, 'You look every whit as lovely as you did when we both stood in that fearsome courtroom.'

He answered all the questions that she poured out about everybody and he reassured her again and again that the child was in no danger, and they both laughed as he described how indignant Buckingham had been and how all London was full of merriment at the trick she had played and delighted at her escape, and that she had been much talked of. Lady Hatton had been questioned and her house searched and Sir Edward's premises were ransacked. He, Robert, had been in prison, but even there he was not above suspicion.

Buckingham's wife, the unfortunate Duchess, had been with him in Portsmouth and saw from a balcony her husband lying dead in the courtyard below. She was heavily pregnant and it was wondered how this incident would affect the child.

Robert had been imprisoned for five months and was still carefully watched after his release, and it was only in the general turmoil after Buckingham's death that he had dared to leave London, but he could not stay long and allow his absence to be noticed.

Whilst the country rejoiced King Charles mourned and found it almost unbearable that his people were so happy at the death of the person he loved so dearly and on whom he had come to depend. He was acting as though he had lost half of himself, and there were fears for his mind. He had taken the Duke's children to be brought up with his own and he counted as his personal enemies all those who had injured Buckingham.

'I fear,' said Robert, 'that you and I are among those enemies. He dare not touch me because I am a Member of Parliament, but should you return I would fear for your safety. Are you happy here?' Frances hesitated and held out her hands to him. He took them and looked hard at her, then asked, 'Are you comfortable – do Gwyneth and Huw look after you?' 'Oh yes, oh yes, they are kindness itself and Tom too sees to my safety and I have all I need and I am not afraid, but it is so lonely here. They speak no English and I have only a few words of Welsh and I do miss my friends and Whitehall and the court and with Buckingham gone I could be so happy. Dare I not return?' Robert shook his head and assured her that in his dreadful grief, King Charles might punish her savagely and would surely re-arrest her. 'He fears and dislikes your father, and your mother is no longer at court, and with all my love I cannot protect you in London. It makes me happy to know you are safe and it is only here that I can do anything for you.'

They had some wonderful days together, riding in the hills and dining on Gwyneth's delicious meals, and he promised to return and above all to tell her when and if she dared return to London. Then all too soon she watched him, tall and handsome, turning to wave to her before he disappeared into the forest and Gwyneth found her in tears.

She tried to busy herself. She picked blackberries, made jams and compots, collected eggs and searched for useful herbs on the hillside and often wished that she had paid better attention to the work in the gardens at Stoke Poges. Each day she learnt a few more words of Welsh. Robert came occasionally, but still advised her not to return yet. He brought her a dappled grey mare and she grew bolder in riding around the hills, but she felt a deep melancholy as she rode in solitude along the paths where she had trotted so gaily with Robert at her side.

It was many months later that Tom appeared with two horsemen and knocked at the parlour door to ask her whether she recognized the men and explained that they said they had been sent by her father to fetch her to his home at Stoke Poges. Tom feared that it might be a ruse to capture her, so he had come himself to make sure that the messengers were genuine and that she was willing to accompany them. She was touched by his solicitude as he handed her a letter and she recognized at once her father's handwriting. It was short and peremptory, saying that he had had a fall from his horse, that he was injured and bade her return to Stoke Poges to look after him. She nodded to Tom to assure him that the message was genuine and asked him to explain to Gwyneth and Huw that she would be leaving and the reason for her departure.

It never occurred to her to question her father's behest, as her awe of him was too deeply ingrained to do other than obey, nor did she ever question whether her safety would be in doubt.

The Duty of a Daughter

Frances rode away from the Hall of the Forest on her own beautiful dappled grey mare, accompanied by the two servants that her father had sent to fetch her. It was quite a change from the way she had arrived and she recalled with distaste the desperate urgency of her flight from London, riding almost day and night for fear of pursuit. This time she could travel more leisurely, stay at good inns and take a more direct route. She felt little anxiety now. Charles was King, the Duke of Buckingham was dead, and his son, born posthumously, had succeeded to the dukedom, so her own Robert was no longer any threat. Her unkind mother-in-law, the Countess, was also dead, so too was the odious Sir Edward Villiers who had so unforgivably manhandled her. Finally, she had total confidence that her father was powerful enough to protect her.

As they left, she glanced back at the old farmhouse that

had been her refuge, nestling among the dark trees and surrounding hills. She could just see the geese preening themselves around the edge of the pond and above she saw the windows of her bedroom on the upper floor, where she had so often looked out with melancholy at the beautiful hillside. It had been a safe remote asylum and she had said her farewells in passable Welsh, with real gratitude for the kindness of Gwyneth and Huw, but she left without the least regret. It had been a desolate, lonely existence, a tranquil living tomb.

The journey took her through Ludlow where they stayed the first night, and as was her wont, she went to pray and entered the beautiful Church of St. Laurence. As she walked around, she paused at the memorial erected by Sir Philip Sydney to his little daughter, Ambrosia, and thought with joy of her own stranger son whom she would now surely see after so long an absence. She knelt to utter a few words of thanksgiving and an urgent prayer for happiness in which she might be close to her child again, perhaps live with her beloved Robert, then she quickly removed that thought from her prayer in case it might be displeasing to God.

The journey continued peacefully and it seemed strange to ride in under the iron gateway of her old home after so long and use the bedroom that she had had as a child. She noted with pleasure that the hangings had not been altered.

Her father had greeted her gruffly without any show of emotion or affection. He had greatly aged and he was often in pain, walking slowly with a stick to help him, but he had become no less harsh with advancing age, and when she suggested the possibility of her child joining her, he was adamant that no adulterous brat would enter his house and assured her that she should give up all thoughts of harlotry, for she was here to look after him and nothing else. It was an unhappy homecoming and Frances fled the room disconsolately at his harsh words; she had seen very little of her father since her marriage long ago and she still stood profoundly in awe of him. Now he worked at his papers all day long and only joined her at meal times when he often ate in silence. She was now in charge of his household and he expected everything to measure up to his exacting standards.

She soon understood that not only would a child's presence vex him, but that no child could be happy in such an austere household and strict regime, and she kept secret her desolation that even now she could not have her son beside her, but she never mentioned the matter again. However she could send letters and messages to him at Corfe, where his grandmother sometimes visited, and where Mistress Wells was still with him.

Compared with life at court it was still a lonely life for Frances, but there were neighbours now, some of whom she had known as a child; she rode most days, and instead of the lonely beauty of Clun she could now visit the parson's wife, nod to the farmers, take help to the sick and attend church. Sometimes there were visitors from London who brought news of that beautiful lost world of Whitehall and the court.

Best of all, she was able to hear from Robert without her father's knowledge, and although he was not welcome to visit, he wrote to her constantly and they began to plan a possible future together. They hoped to get an annulment of her marriage on the grounds of John's mental instability, and they discussed turning back to the Catholic faith in their bitterness at the harsh treatment they had received from the Church of England which had publicly excommunicated Robert and sentenced her to penance. Queen Henrietta, the staunchest of Catholics, with the heart and ear of the King, would surely entreat for annulment of Frances' marriage.

These plans kept her hopes high as her father grew steadily weaker in body, but he remained strong in mind and in temper, growing more demanding and keeping her ever closer to tend to his needs. He would see no doctor, nor take any physic, saying that he now had a disease which 'all the drugs of Asia, the gold of Africa, nor all the doctors of Europe could cure – old age'.

Despite his years and infirmity, he was still regarded with suspicion in high places. When it was discovered that he was writing a book, King Charles was alarmed and one of his courtiers wrote of it: 'in the which the King fears that somewhat may be to the prejudice of his prerogative for he (Coke) is held in too great an oracle among the people and they may be misled by anything that carries such an authority as all things doth that he either speaks or writes, for the prevention of which His Majesty thinks it fit the book should not come forth.' This was surely a magnificent, if unwilling, testimony to the regard in which Coke was generally held as a most stalwart upholder of justice. Sir Frances Winwood, Secretary of State, was sent to search the house for the book and for any other treasonable documents, but when he arrived Sir Edward was too ill to receive him, too ill even to be aware of his presence. His room was thoroughly searched and all his papers were gathered together and taken away, but nothing incriminating was found. On 3rd September 1634 Sir Edward died and the general verdict on him was that he was 'one of the most disagreeable men of his time, but that he was the most incorruptible judge in a period of exceptional corruption'.

Frances did not grieve unduly for her formidable father, but as she followed his coffin to the church of Stoke Poges and to burial in Norfolk, she realized that she was now homeless and quite poor. The house belonged to her mother, and all ten children of Sir Edward's first marriage hurried to claim what they could. Frances' sister Elizabeth had died, but her two children also demanded their share, as Frances had received (and lost to the Villiers) a large dowry, so now her portion was but a pittance.

At last, however, it was wonderful to be able to meet Robert freely, and it was his suggestion that she should return to London where he helped her find a small house on the south bank of the Thames, just across from Westminster, not far from Lambeth, and here Frances began to feel alive again. She sent for her son, and she dreamt of an annulment of her marriage and perhaps even a union with Robert. With joy her many friends welcomed her back; she was thirty two now, still beautiful, witty and always merry; she had caused such scandal and pleasure by outwitting Buckingham that everyone hastened to hear her tell of her adventures; and she hoped daily to be accepted at court. Indeed she felt sure that in due course both the King and the Queen would welcome her. Meanwhile she happily spent her days furnishing her new home, choosing curtain hangings, buying new costumes, visiting and being visited.

She and Robert announced their return to the Roman Catholic faith intending to seek an annulment of Frances' marriage on account of John's mental instability, by-passing the increasingly puritanical and implacable Church of England and hoping that Queen Henrietta, a fervent Roman Catholic, would help them. Neither Frances nor Robert ever expected the trouble that was awaiting them and made no attempt to hide their meetings, and all too often a barge, rowed by men in the navy-blue serge Suffolk livery, was seen crossing the Thames to the south bank. Frances had no barge herself, but it was easy to hire a boatman and there was much coming and going. They had failed to understand the utter desolation felt by the King at the assassination of Buckingham. Unlike his father, who had a violent temper but no rancour, Charles could never forgive nor forget, but bore his grudges for ever. He still considered that Frances had harmed and humiliated Buckingham and he now determined to bring her once again to justice.

The sequel is told all too vividly in a letter from Archbishop Laud to a fellow prelate. 'Sir Robert Howard and Lady Purbeck grew to such boldness that he brought her to London and lodged her in Westminster so near the court and in so open a view that the King and the Lordes took notice of it as a thing full of impudence that they should so publicly advernture to outface the Justice of the Realm in so fowl a business. One day His Majesty took me aside and added it was a great reproach to the Church and Nation and that I neglected my duty in case I did not take order for it. I made answer that she was a wife of a Peere of the Realm and that without his leave I could not attach her. Now I know his pleasure I would do my best to have her taken and brought to Penance. The next day I had the good hap to apprehend both her and Sir Robert and by order of the High Commission Court imprisoned her in the

Gate House and him in the Fleet. This was a Wednesday and Sunday sennight after was thought upon to bring her to Penance. She was much troubled and so was he.'

Frances was more than troubled, she was devastated and could not believe that ecclesiastical vengeance could have lasted for so many years. Once more she was a subject of pity and gossip, some malicious. Churchmen as a whole felt pleased that the authority of the Church should be upheld and that she should not escape the punishment imposed upon her for presumed adultery, even after such a length of time.

A local clergyman wrote: 'Lady Purbeck had evaded sentence by flight and had not been much looked after since, but this winter she lodged herself on the water side, over against Lambeth, I fear too near the road of the Archbishops guards, whereof some complaint being made, he had the Sargeant at Arms sent with a warrant of the Lord of the Council to carry her to the Gate House where she will hardly get out until she has done her penance. The same night a warrant to the Warden of the Fleet to take Sir Robert Howard at Suffolk House.'

A Fugitive Again

Frances sat on the straw pallet in a small cell. It was dimly lit by a window high in the wall and she buried her face in her hands until, as she confessed later, 'My eyes were so swollen with blubbering that I could neither see nor hear.'

Indeed she did not hear her cell door open. She had been three days in prison and the time was approaching when she would be taken out for penance. The gaoler stood for a second or two looking down on her bowed head in silence. 'My lady' he said at last. She looked up quickly, fearfully – surely the dreaded moment had not yet arrived. 'My lady,' he repeated, 'can I help you?'

Frances shook her head. 'No-one can help me now.' Then she suddenly added, 'Indeed you can help me. I would sooner take my life than endure that penance. Bring me a potion that will kill me, send me to sleep for ever. I will see that you are well recompensed.'

'That I will not, my Lady. You are too young and too fair, but I will help you to disappear. I am old now and I have been a gaoler here for many a year. I was here when you were first brought to court and you but a child so ill-treated by that evil Duke.'

'What is your name?' enquired Frances in astonishment.

'Aquila Weekes, my Lady. Could you hide somewhere safely if you got out of here?'

Frances paused, lost in amazement, and then murmured, almost thinking aloud, 'I would have to go further than Clun this time. They would seek me there or at Hatton House or Stoke Poges, or,' and she hesitated, 'Corfe Castle. I must go further, abroad perhaps. I could go to Guernsey where the Governor is a relation of mine and he would surely help me and nobody would think of looking for me there.' She looked up almost hopefully. 'My uncle is Governor of Portsmouth and he would surely help me board a ship.'

There was very little time to lose, so that very day a messenger was sent to Lord Wimbledon, Governor of Portsmouth, horses were acquired from Hatton House, and friends supplied Frances with a boy's tunic and hose. Her long fair hair was tucked under a cap that hid much of her face.

Once plans were laid, Frances was in a fever of anxiety lest anything untoward should stop her escape. On the Friday evening, thirty-six hours before her Sunday penance was due, it fell out that there were more visitors to the prison than usual, and that evening as they left a young lad emerged with them and passed unnoticed among the departing crowd. Frances was a fugitive once more. Again, she did not know who was to accompany her or how her escape was to be accomplished, but as she passed out of the prison gates, her arm was firmly taken by a young man and she was led swiftly to a side street where two horses were waiting.

It was better weather this time, but the journey started at night and Frances had perforce to ride astride. She found it almost impossible to swing her leg over the saddle and she longed for the familiar pummel that held her so safely on her mount, but with no time to spare her companion pushed her unceremoniously up into the saddle and she clung to her horse's mane until she gradually grew used to the strange position.

They did not leave London for several days, but lay low and waited until the first hubbub had subsided. Now her hair was cut quite short and in her brown hose and tunic and boy's cap, it would have been impossible to recognise her as Viscountess Lady Purbeck. On the ride to Portsmouth, no-one gave a second look at the young lad riding carefree on an old nag.

She was received by her uncle, Lord Wimbledon, with no very good will. It was only at his sister's urgent plea that he had agreed to help after Lady Hatton had arranged the escort from London. This niece of his had spelt trouble for most of her married life and he was only anxious to send her on her way without his involvement becoming known.

When she entered his house in her hose and tunic, he winced and exclaimed, 'Zounds, child, cover yourself up decently,' and found her a cloak. Both he and Frances were anxious that she should be on her way. Within a week he managed to arrange a passage for her on a small ship sailing to Guernsey and she left, still dressed in male attire. He sent an old attendant to accompany her, but never divulged who she was, merely telling him to see the youth to the Governor's residence and leave him there.

They took up cramped quarters towards the stern of the ship and looked out over a dismally grey squally sea, but the wind was so strong and contrary that it was twenty-four hours before they could get out of port. It was an abominable journey with mountainous seas and the ship rolled fearsomely. Frances' escort, a very reluctant sailor, kept muttering that he couldn't see why a youth couldn't make the journey alone, and as his seasickness grew, so his discontent mounted.

The journey lasted nearly a week, and whilst the sailors laughed at the discomfiture of their passengers, there were moments when even Frances wondered whether penance would have been more painful. When at last they arrived and stepped off the gangway, her companion fell to the ground on the shore and vowed that, God willing, should he get back safely to Portsmouth, he would never leave dry land again. He pointed in the direction of the residence, told Frances to make her way there and closed his eyes.

Frances too felt queasy and was still embarrassed at walking about in men's hose in public, feeling that people were staring at her, but she looked at the prostrate figure of her escort, bade him farewell and walked firmly in the direction he had pointed. There was a large almost empty square before the Governor's residence and she started to circle round it, but after a while, when nobody seemed to give her a second look, she resolutely crossed the square and mounted the imposing flight of steps leading to the front door. She pulled the bell chain and waited. After a while, the door opened and a magnificently attired footman looked down at her in silence. Frances looked down at her dirty hose and when the flunkey suggested that she should go to the servants' door, she meekly complied. There they enquired about her errand, and when she asked to see the Governor privately, they looked astonished and very doubtful. The Governor, they assured her, was busy and might be going out presently, but by now she had courage enough to say with a little asperity that she had a message for him from a friend in London

It was not until some hours later that she was admitted to his presence, and even then there were two clerks present. Frances repeated her request to speak to him privately and he looked at his guest quizzically. So frail and unmenacing a youth could hardly be plotting an assassination, so he dismissed the clerks and bade the lad hurry with his message as he had work to do.

'Frances Coke, Frances Purbeck,' he repeated again and again in his agitation, disinclined to believe it as she explained her disguise and her desperate plight. He showed only too clearly that he was dismayed beyond measure. A rather sanctimonious bachelor, he had no wish whatsoever to become embroiled with his cousin and her unsavoury conduct. He certainly did not wish to offend the King or risk his career. He walked to and fro in disarray.

Eventually he offered her suitable woman's clothing and even gave her a little money, hoping that that would not be reported back to Whitehall, but he was adamant that she could not remain in Guernsey. When she suggested that no-one would look for her there, he replied curtly that it was out of the question. Guernsey was a small island, her presence would be quickly reported and he could not guarantee her safety, nor, he added, condone her conduct. Frances was dismayed, but he was not to be moved. For once her charm failed and he had no answer when she begged him to advise her what she should do next.

It was clear that he would have preferred to send her back to carry out her penance, but this he could not quite bring himself to do. 'You must leave the island immediately,' he insisted. 'Either you must return to England, and I understand your reluctance, or you must go to France and I will assist you to get to Paris where you will surely find friends in the English community there.'

For Frances there was no choice, and all too soon she was on board a boat to France and then on her way to Paris. She had acquaintances there and ignominiously had to beg their help, and with their advice she took a small house not far from the Embassy. She was quickly introduced into the English colony, but her fame had spread before her and it was not long before everyone came to call and she had to recite her adventures again and again. She was torn between feelings of elation at once more having eluded authority and acute anxiety as to her future.

She was distressingly poor, so she only engaged two servants, a French maid and a manservant, and she settled down to wait. Robert would come to Paris as soon as he was released and they might then live abroad, but they still fervently hoped for a pardon for Frances and an annulment of her marriage on account of John's illness, so that they might return to England as man and wife.

Her anxiety turned to panic when she learnt that King Charles was in no mood to let her slip away and make a mockery of him once again. She found that he had sent an express messenger with a summons signed with the Great Seal ordering her to return to England forthwith. Disobedience would be treason, a far more serious offence than anything she had done so far, and if she failed to answer the summons, she could never return to England again.

It was essential that the messenger did not find her to deliver the summons, so she barred her doors and windows and told her servants never to admit anyone they did not know. She never went out without a suitable escort and she only received her friends at home.

Yet again, Frances was the subject of gossip and interest, both in Paris and in London, and a local clergyman wrote: 'Another has gone over to that Popish religion, Sir Robert Howard, which I am sorry for. My Lady Purbeck has left her country and her religion both together and since he will not cease thinking of her, but live in that detestable sin, let him go to that Church for absolution, for he can find none in ours.'

Whilst Frances was trying to ensure her own safety, she had no inkling of the trouble she was causing at the English Embassy and if she had, it would have done nothing to assuage her fears. Viscount Scudamore, the Ambassador, had formerly been a member of the Council of the Marches and had undoubtedly heard of the fugitive of Clun, and like

Lord Danby of Guernsey, he had no wish to jeopardise his career. His abject letter to the Secretary of State tells the whole episode.

'Rt. Honble, Your letter dated the 7th March – I received the 21 the same style by the Courier sent to serve His Majesties writ upon the Lady Viscountess Purbeck. They came to me about 12 of the clock in the morning. Upon the instant of his coming to me, I sent a servant of mjyne own to show him the house where the Lady lived publiqyely, and in my neighbourhood. In arriving at the house where Lady Purbeck was living, the Courier taking off his Messenger's badge, knocked at the door to get in. There came a Mayde to the door that would not open it, but peeped through a grating and asked his business. He sayd he was not in such haste, but would come back againe tomorrow. But the Mayde and the rest of the household having charge not to open the doore but to suche as were well knowne the Messenger could not get in.'

By now the Ambassador and the Messenger were anxious lest Frances should slip away and they began to treat the matter with great urgency. The letter continues: 'We endeavoured by severall ways to have gotten the Messenger into the house. But having considered and tried until the next afternoon, we grew very doubtful that the Messenger might be suspected and that the Lady might slip away from that place of residence by night.

Therefore I directed the Bearer to put the boxe with the Privy Seale in it through some pane of a lower window into the house and leaving it there to put on his Badge and knocking at the door of the house, it they would not suffer him to enter, then to tell that party who should speak to him at the doore, that he was sent from the King of Grate Britaine to serve His Majsties Privy Seale upon the Lady Viscountess Purbeck and that in regard he could not be admitted in, he had left the Privy Seale in a box in such a place in the house and that in His Majesties name, he required the Lady Purbeck to take notice thereof at her peril.'

This was no easy task since all doors and ground floor windows were closed fast, but finally the Ambassador was able to report success and his letter continued: 'The Messenger being there, found an upper window neath the casements and threw up the boxe with the Privy Seale in it through the window into a chamber which some say is the Lady's bedroom, others that it is the chamber of the man servant waiting upon her.'

There was never any requirement upon the Messenger to arrest Frances, but only to serve the writ validly. However the Messenger, in his pleasure at his success, forgot his second duty which was to announce to anyone at the door that the writ was in the house.

Back went the Messenger, and the Ambassador continued: 'The Courier returned to me and finding that he had forgotten to speke at the doore as I had directed him, I caused him presently to return and to discharge himself in such sort as is above mentioned.'

Still they had no actual proof that Frances was in the house and the Ambassador, desperate to show his zeal in carrying out the King's orders, now devised a plan to ascertain her presence, and wrote about 'a woman being sent to the house under colour of speaking with the Ladies servant, the Ladye herself came to the doore and opening it a little soe that the woman saw her, she sayd that her sister should have leave to go home to her that night. And therefore the Ladye was in the house at the same time that the place of her residence was served.'

Viscount Scudamore was not yet free of the inconvenience caused by this unwelcome visitor, because the very next day he wrote again: 'The morrow after the writ was served, about midnight there came some officers with two coaches and 50 archers to divers houses to search for the Lady Purbeck, being directed and instructed by the Cardinal Richelieu that whereas there was a Messenger sent from England to offer some affront to the Lady Purbeck in diminution of the King's jurisdiction that therefore they should find the sayd ladye and protect her. Coming to the knowledge of this particular I thought good to hasten the

Messenger out of the way.'

Frances was in diplomatic trouble once more. France was staunchly Catholic, and as a recent convert to that faith, the King and Queen might welcome her as a persecuted religious refugee. Cardinal Richelieu was always delighted to embarrass England and this was a welcome opportunity.

When Frances had received the writ and learnt that French troops were seeking to protect her, she wept and could not conceive what to do next. She had no wish to find herself in permanent exile through disobedience, yet she utterly refused to return to do that penance, nor did she wish to live on the charity of the French court.

Each day she hoped to see Robert or at least hear from him, but then she had news from a friend of his that he was still held in close confinement and that the only terms on which he would be released would be for him to sign a pledge 'never to come at the Ladye again'. Furthermore he must agree to appear at Whitehall at any time within forty-eight hours of being summoned, which precluded him from leaving the country. Charles was truly unforgiving.

Sir Kenelm Digby, who was one of the English émigrés living in Paris and who had been greatly touched by Frances' predicament, happened to call that day and found Frances in deep despair. He sat and comforted her and then finally made the wise suggestion that she should take refuge in a convent and he knew the Reverend Mother in the English Convent in Paris. There even King Charles could not reach her, for a holy lady in a holy place did not need immediately to heed the command to return and she might rest there awhile in peace whilst a permanent solution was sought.

It was good advice which Frances accepted gratefully. She even spoke of taking the veil, but she was quickly aware that the Reverend Mother did not approve of her. Her reputation had gone before her and no nun could condone adultery, and Frances soon found that convent life was not a happy one. She found her cell very uncomfortable, the cold was terrible and the food was bad and in short supply and she was subject to many petty convent rules. It was not the sanctuary for which she had hoped.

Frances tried to adjust to monastic rules, but it seemed to her that life went from one unhappy state to another, from the misery of Buckingham's persecution to the loneliness of Clun, thence to her morose father, and when for one instant everything seemed just about to go right, she was persecuted again, and convent life seemed uninviting. After a few months, the Reverend Mother decided that she was unsuitable even as a temporary lodger in a convent and by mutual consent she left. She was destitute now, dependent on friends and occasional sums of money from England.

The matter was discussed in high places and a letter from Sir Thomas Puckeridge, a Member of Parliament, states, 'The last week we had certain news that the Ladye Purbeck was declared a Papist. The French King and Queen and the eminent Cardinal Richelieu have sent messages to King Charles to pardon my Ladye Purbeck and to allow her to return to England. The French Ambassador at St. James's is verie zealous in the business. It is said that she is altogether advised by Sir Kenelm Digby who hath written over letters to some of his noble friends of the Privy Council, wherein he hath set down what a Converte this Ladye is become, so superlatively virtuous and sanctimonious as the like hath never been seen in Man or Woman and therefore he does most humbly desire their Lordships to farther the Ladye's cause and that she may return to England for otherwise she does resolve to put herself into some Monastery. I hear that his Majesty doth most utterly dislike that the ladye is so directed by Sir Kenelm Digby and that she fares no better for it.'

Sir Kenelm's father had been involved in the Gunpowder Plot, so he was mistrusted by the King, but nevertheless he worked tirelessly on Frances' behalf. He wrote letters to many of his friends, including one to her uncle Lord Wimbledon. 'Truly, my Lord, I have not seen more prudence, sweetness, goodness, honour and bravery shewed by any woman that I know than this unfortunate Ladye sheweth she hath a rich stock of. Besides her natural endowments doubtless her afflictions add much or rather have polished, refined and heightened what nature gave her and you know *vexatio dat intellectum*. Is it not a shame for you Peeres (and near about the King) that you will let so brave a Ladye live as she does in disttress and banishment when her exile serveth stronger but to conceive scandalously of our nation that we will not permit those to live among us who have so much worth and goodness as this ladye giveth show of.'

As a student, Sir Kenelm had had Archibishop Laud as his tutor and they had become friends so he hoped a letter to him might persuade the Archbishop to grant a pardon, probably not realizing that it was King Charles himself who was unforgiving.

Grudgingly, after much persuasion from the King and Queen of France, from Cardinal Richelieu and the French Ambassador at St. James, Charles issued a pardon for her penance and withdrew his order for her immediate return – indeed it was some months before he allowed this and then only on one condition, that she must come back as John Villiers' wife. It was a cruel decree. Sir Robert had only been released from prison on condition that he signed a pledge of £2,000 agreeing 'never to come at the lady again'. Frances might return, but they could never be together.

She looked round her rented rooms, for she now had no money to rent a house, and thought bitterly that this was her hated brother-in-law Buckingham's final triumph over her from beyond the grave, and her mind was in turmoil. She and Robert had so firmly believed that, as Catholics, an annulment might be obtained, and now she must return to John after so many years that she had been forced to keep away from him; and yet she knew that she should feel gratitude to John for agreeing to take her back and also to the King for his pardon, allowing her to return even on such exacting terms.

She confided her sorrow to Sir Kenelm. He was silent for a while then raised her hand to his lips, and with tears in his eyes he advised her to accept these cruel terms. All Paris would miss her and he was desolate, but she could not live happily for ever alone and in penury. England was her home and there lived her child, her mother, her lover, her husband and the life to which she had always been accustomed.

Homecoming

With fearful misgivings, Frances set out for Calais to take ship to England. For once, she almost hoped for shipwreck, footpads, a mishap on the coach or at least contrary winds, but the journey was swift and easy. The Channel was calm and slightly misty, with just sufficient breeze to carry the ship gently on its way, and all too soon as the clouds lifted, the great white cliffs of England appeared. John did not meet her himself, but he sent his coach and servants to bring her to Whitehall, where as Buckingham's brother, he was still granted an apartment.

It was a strange moment and her heart was beating fast as she was ushered into John's presence and she saw him once again. She curtsied low and long, hardly daring to look up at him, but he took her hand and lifted her up. 'Frances,' he said softly and she wept. He had aged, his hair was grizzled and sparser, his face was lined, both by age and by illness, but he accepted her without reproach, and he never mentioned the past, nor spoke about his brother Buckingham or the cruelty he had shown them; he acted as if those long years had vanished. He was always gentle and courteous to her, but there was a change. When he had fallen ill long years ago, he had been put into the care of Dr. Innocent Lamier and Frances realized that a real friendship had grown up between the two men. And whereas previously John had always confided and relied on her, now she felt that the doctor was his prime confidant.

Her next ordeal was to beg an audience with the King. He kept her waiting for many days, then she kissed his hand to thank him for his pardon and for his permission to return to court. He looked long at her and she dropped her eyes – there was no smile or loving kindness in his gaze, he merely acknowledged her obeisance with cold courtesy and she knew that nothing had been forgotten or forgiven.

It was quite different when she curtsied to the Queen who smiled sweetly, for Frances was a welcome convert to her own Catholic religion, and it was due to her and to her brother, the King of France, that Frances had been pardoned. As a gawky, unsophisticated bride of fourteen, Henrietta Maria, on leaving Paris to become Charles' bride, was told by her confessor that it was her God-given mission to bring England back to Roman Catholicism; she had been so embarrassingly fervent in her childish enthusiasm for this that her marriage had been in danger of breakdown – she even refused to attend the coronation because it was a Protestant ceremony. Charles had angrily sent all her French servants back to France and she had sulked alone in her own apartments, whilst he had neglected her and enjoyed Buckingham's friendship. Only after Buckingham's murder and his subsequent loneliness and emotional anguish had he turned to his Queen for comfort. Then the marriage had become a happy one and her influence became as strong as Buckingham's had been, but with equally unfortunate consequences, because as a Catholic she was deeply unpopular with the English people.

Frances realized that, with the Queen's approval and so long as she was never seen with Sir Robert Howard, she had little to fear and she tried to fit in to the court circle once more. She sent for her son, but Robert was now a self-possessed youth of twelve, quite a stranger to his mother, and his talk was all of Corfe Castle, hawking and his Lady Grandmother. Frances mourned for the lost years in which she had played no part in his life and she felt sorrowful and estranged, both from her husband and her child.

Whitehall and the court were also astonishingly different and the coarse merry bawdiness of King James was no more. A contemporary tells how 'King Charles was temperate and chaste and serious, so that the fools and bawds, mimicks and catamites of the former court grew out of fashion and the nobilitie and courtiers, who did not quite abandon their debosheries, had yet that reverence to the King to retire into corners to practice them.'

Frances often saw Robert and they exchanged formal greetings, but they never dared speak to each other privately because they knew that spies were all around them and would surely report any breach of Sir Robert's undertaking. They looked at each other across the room, their glances met in Church, but their hands never clasped, their lips never met and their constant propinquity tortured them.

Not only the court, but England also had changed. King Charles had ruled for eleven years without calling Parliament and its members were resentful and ready to oppose him fiercely. He had antagonized everyone – country landowners by imposing stringent illegal taxation, towns which had to produce forced loans and ship money – and he had meddled with the liberties of the City of London. He seemed to have disassociated himself from his subjects and shut himself away in Whitehall where he collected magnificent works of art, and despite his financial difficulties, he put on extravagant and costly masques. Frances watched one, staged by the genius Inigo Jones, in which Charles appeared as a victorious and beloved monarch and she marvelled at a scene in which Henrietta and her ladies appeared in a 'cloud of surpassing beauty'.

Out of touch with reality, Charles in no wise sensed the danger behind the growing animosity of most of his subjects. Crisis point was reached when he interfered with the Scottish religion and angry Scots marched south, occupied Newcastle and Durham and refused to retreat until they were paid substantial sums of money. Then Charles in his penury had no option but to summon Parliament and demand money. When it refused him, he prorogued it and arrested some of its members. Still in desperate financial need, he recalled Parliament once more and this time the members locked themselves in so that he was unable to dismiss them. They presented him with the Grand Remonstrance outlining their many grievances and insisting that he attend to them before money matters could be discussed.

Growing braver, they impeached his chief military commander, the Earl of Strafford, and demanded that the King sign his death warrant. When he hesitated, for Strafford had been a good and loyal servant to him, there was alarming rioting, and the city closed the shops in panic, apprentices joined the rioters with alacrity and a great crowd surged round Whitehall. Terrified courtiers confessed themselves to the Queen's chaplain, sharpened their swords and discussed where and how they might make a stand against the mob. Still the King hesitated to sign and a tense night followed.

The next day fresh rioters appeared and everyone listened in fear to the roar of the crowd outside, until at last at 9 o'clock on Sunday evening, 12th May 1639, with tears in his eyes, Charles signed the death warrant and Strafford went to his execution. The King never forgave himself and referred to this occasion when later he himself stood on the scaffold.

Frances and John had listened in fear to the militant mob outside. Her son Robert was at Hatton House with his grandmother where it was safer, for the anger of the mob was directed at the King and even more against the Queen because of her Popish influence.

And then the King made one more error – this time a fatal one. In an effort to reassert his authority, he rode to Parliament at the head of a troop of cavalry to arrest the ringleaders, but Parliament barred its doors against him and he found that by using force against his people, he had combined the wrath of everyone – the City of London, the Lords and Parliament. London became so hostile and untenable that he slipped away to continue the struggle from York.

It was a perplexing time for everybody, but especially for Frances with no-one to guide her. She had no doubt but that the King would quickly subdue his unruly subjects and it never occurred to her to side with Parliament. The same could be said for most of the nobility and many started to go north to stand beside their King, whilst their ladies mostly went back to their country estates, but Frances had nowhere to go and she had to think of her son Robert who was now of an age to enlist, yet he seemed strangely disinclined to do so. He spent much time with Lady Hatton and one day he announced that she was siding with Parliament and that he was considering it.

Frances was outraged and angry words were exchanged with her mother. She accused her of ruining her life by agreeing to her unhappy marriage, and now that she had a son who would inherit a title and who was acknowledged by John, he was being suborned by her from following his King. Lady Hatton would not be executed for treason, but a young man might well be and in any case he would lose lands, title and honour.

When Lady Hatton then suggested that Parliament might win, Frances shook her head in exasperation and quickly found Robert a commission with the King's forces. John was obviously unfit to fight, unfit in mind and body, and he happily returned to live with his friend and guardian, Dr. Innocent Lamier.

Frances' mind was finally made up when Parliamentarians ransacked her house and took her goods, and in company with several other ladies, she took a coach and joined the court at Oxford.

War

Once King Charles raised his standard on 2nd August 1642, war became inevitable because anybody who opposed him was then guilty of treason.

The first task for both sides was to commandeer arms. There was no regular standing army, but each county kept a store of armour, pikes, muskets, balls and gunpowder in its own store. Parliament, the City of London and Hull all declared for the anti-monarchy Puritans. Oxford was indecisive, inclining to the Puritans, but Archbishop Laud was Chancellor of the University and he naturally opted for the King, so Oxford shortly became the Royalist Headquarters, and even a Parliament of sorts was set up there.

It was a shocking change for a university town, particularly as the townsfolk sided very reluctantly with the Royalists.

The King occupied Christ Church, the Queen's party were in Merton, twenty guns were parked near Magdalen, Law and Logic Schools became granaries, the powder mill was in the ruins of Osney Abbey and the great quad of Christ Church held a drove of fat oxen and 300 sheep. Work was started on the fortifications, and townsmen were ordered to do one day's work a week, which they carried out grudgingly.

The Acting Vice-Chancellor ordered a show of arms when he heard of an approaching Parliamentarian force. Anthony Wood, then aged twelve, wrote a graphic account of what happened in his household. His father had armour for one man, viz. helmet, back and breast piece, pike, musket and other appurtenances. The senior of three men servants, Thomas Burnham, wore these when training was ordered, but if he was too busy, then the second servant took his place.

Scholars were far too interested watching soldiers drill and their lessons suffered abominably. There were quaint Oxford dons, amongst them the picturesque figure of Dr. Kettle who cared very little about the war, but waged his own battle against what he termed 'hairy locks'. He carried a muff against the cold and therein he hid his scissors, whipping them out to cut any locks that offended him. One day, being without his usual scissors, he seized the bread knife used to cut the students' loaves and happily used that instead.

When the King rode in after the victory at Edge Hill, all the church bells rang out and there was great jubilation. This was in October and everybody expected to be back in Whitehall by Christmas, but Christmas came and went and victory still eluded the King.

At first it was all rather like a delightful prolonged picnic. Cavaliers and their ladies would meet in New College Gardens and it was here that Lady Thynne and her friend Mrs. Fanshawe decided to play a practical joke on Dr. Kettle. They dressed like 'angels' (prostitutes) and called on him, but he was not amused. 'Your husband and your father I knew,' he thundered. 'I know you to be gentlewomen and I will not say that you are whores, but get you gone, get you gone for a very woman.'

Frances took lodgings near Merton where she could walk to meet her friends each day. Sir Robert was among those who rode in with the King and for a few blissful days they were together, at last free and unafraid. Now that war had broken out, no-one had the time or inclination to worry about them or spy on them and although it was only for a few days, they were days and nights of joy. All too soon Robert had to leave again to take part in the siege of Bristol. As he left her with a parting kiss, he swore that he would fight so valiantly for the King that he would surely reward him by granting Frances an annulment and then they could be together for ever.

Oxford grew accustomed to military life, to drums, to the clatter of horses on the cobbled streets, the sound of bells proclaiming victory, the silence of defeat, prisoners brought in bound amid hooting and booing, occasional corpses on the gibbet in Carfax and solemn military funerals.

As the war progressed, there were frequent outbreaks of smallpox and camp fever. The soldiers were blamed as it was said to be 'seldom or never known that an army where there is so much filth, nastiness of diet, worse lodging, unshifted apparel should long continue without contagious disease.'

Life in Oxford gradually became anything but a picnic. A girl named Ann reported: 'My father commanded my sister and me to come to him in Oxford where the court then was. We that had till then lived in great plenty and great order found the scene so changed that we knew not how to act any part but that of obedience. From as good a house as any gentleman in England, we came to a baker's house in an obscure street to lie in an garret, to one dish of meat and that not of the best. We had no money for we were as poor as Job.'

How differently Frances felt. True, the food was poor and scanty and her lodgings were mean, but for her life was joyous. After a successful sortie at Bristol, Robert was sent to hold Donnington, near Newbury, and once again his route brought him through Oxford and they spent a few precious days together, never long, but enough to keep her courage high and her hopes for the future rosy until his next visit.

The whole of England was suffering now in this war that nobody wanted and that nobody seemed able to stop. Lord Spencer wrote a poignant letter to his young wife at Althorp that 'neither is there wanting daily handsome occasions to retire, were it not for grinning honour. Unless a man were resolve to fight on the Parliament side, which for my part I had rather be hanged, it will be said without doubt that a man is afraid to fight.'

Unemployment and poverty were universal. Welsh farmers could not sell their cattle, Gloucestershire clothiers were ruined, in Bristol the markets were deserted, trade was derelict and a quarter of the population died from plague. London too suffered for want of fresh food from the country and coal from Newcastle. Fuel prices soared and the poor perished in the winter cold. The universal prayer was, 'From plundering of soldiers, their insolence, their whores, their cruelty, blasphemy and rule over us, *Libera nos Domine.*'

By August 1643, there were forty deaths a week in Oxford. The accounts of St. Martin, Carfax, record payments for shrouds and grave digging. Soon the churchwardens paid for frankincense and such like to safeguard against infection and to drown the stench of corpses buried too near the surface. Richard Baxter, the preacher, wrote: 'Oh the sad heart piercing spectacles that mine eyes have seen these past years space; scarce a month, scarce a week without the sight or noise of blood.'

With all this suffering, Frances was almost ashamed of her own happiness and peace of mind. In January Robert appeared unexpectedly. He entered her shabby rooms and after their first joyful greeting, he looked round sadly. 'How we are all sunk,' he said. Frances only laughed and repeated that these were the happiest days of her life – no fears, no threats from Church or State or relatives and a wonderful future together. She looked at him seriously. 'I know that you too have suffered, you have been held in prison, you were excommunicated and publicly humiliated, but you cannot understand the relief I feel.'

Robert gently kissed her hair. 'My own love, I do know and I have suffered with you and felt double pain because I could not help you.' But Frances interrupted him and, as if by cataloguing all the horrors she had endured she might rid herself of them, said, 'For twenty-two years since I was fifteen I lived in fear, sometimes for my life, for as you know brother Buckingham hired assassins to kill me and my child, they stole my dowry, they stole my jewellery and silver, they refused me access to John and any means of living, but perhaps even worse, for every moment of married life, he and his mother hated me, criticized me and had me watched, so that I could not even trust my own servants, and now for the first time since I left home, I am free. No-one pursues me and the war will surely end soon.'

'Frances,' he said softly and gently took her arm and drew her towards him. 'The King is losing this war.' She stared at him in disbelief. 'But,' she stammered, 'You won at Edgehill, you were successful at Bristol.' 'True,' he nodded, 'we have had some successes, but now 20,000 Scots have entered the war against us. If we look to be defeated, and God knows I will fight with all my force until the very end, but if we are defeated, you and I will lose everything, lands, titles, money. Will you join me and we will live abroad, as we once thought to when you were in Paris? It will be a poor life, a penniless one, but we shall have each other.'

Frances slipped on to her knees before him and took both his hands in hers, and looking up at him, her eyes bright with tears, whispered, 'Oh yes, my love, and gladly. You hold my heart, my life, my happiness in these hands,' and she kissed them. 'For my sake, do not be too brave. Come back for me soon and come safely, my dearest treasure.'

The next day she watched him leave once more, riding proudly at the head of his troop with a cheerful expression and a salute for the cheering crowd and she gazed at him with pride and yearning. To return to her lodging, she had to pass through the filth and misery of the city, but she barely noticed for her heart was exultant. As she reached her small room, she knelt in thankfulness and only prayed that he would not be foolishly brave, that he would return safely to her. '*Ave Maria, Ave Maria, Ore pro nobis*' Blessed Mary, you who knew all the sorrows of life, have mercy on us and bring us together. Guard him in battle, do not let his courage destroy him, bring him back safely to me. Mary, Mother of God, I do not ask for riches or titles or fame – just to be with the man I love.'

Robert left Oxford in sombre mood. He had trotted out gaily at the head of his troop with a smile on his face and a wave for those watching them depart, but his outward gaiety hid a deep depression. Not only was the war going badly for the King with the Scots invading in force and the Puritans constantly gaining ground, but he was distressed at the lack of discipline amongst the Royalist ranks. They caused hardship wherever they went, wherever they were quartered. They plundered and ransacked whole villages, leaving the inhabitants starving and full of rancour; they were increasingly disliked and he sensed that the whole country was turning against them Their opponents might desecrate churches, but they spared people's homes and belongings and their forces were disciplined and paid for what they commandeered.

As he rode, he thought repeatedly of his beloved Frances, radiant and even more beguiling in poverty. He felt moved almost to tears by her constancy and her joy and certainty in their future together and it was born upon him with a tremor of guilt how much his love for her must have contributed to Buckingham's hostility.

Was he, he began to wonder, the cause of her suffering and would she have been happier without him? But he brushed these thoughts from his mind as he recollected that day so long ago when he had been present at her wedding and seen her slight body shaken with sobs. He had felt revolted at the powers that could force a child of fifteen into so unwelcome a match. Later, on one of the many occasions when John was away from the court, he had come across her, alone and unhappy, standing like a waif, too shy to enter the dining hall alone, and he had offered her his arm. The smile she had given him then had captured his heart for ever and he knew deep down that their love for each other was the only certainty in both their lives, and that Frances had needed his support as greatly as he needed her.

Her hair was still golden, her eyes bright and her courage unshaken. Dressed now in faded woollen gowns, with neither ruff nor jewellery, she hardly seemed to notice the squalor of her rooms, nor the wretched food that was all that could be had at present in Oxford. It tore his heart to leave her alone there and he wondered how he could best protect her in the difficult times ahead. It occurred to him that he might bring her somehow to a refuge in Clun, and that the loneliness she had felt there previously might be preferable to a war-torn Oxford. The fight was growing more bitter now and people had suffered too much and too long for anyone to be sure of magnanimity in defeat, whichever side won.

If they had to go into exile, it would be easier if Frances were nearer his lands. He had already heard that all his estates were to be sequestrated and that he was no longer a Member of Parliament in Westminster, but in Shropshire he had friends who would always shelter them until they could slip away abroad.

He felt a suffocating anger at the selfishness of her father who had so casually thrown her away to be the wife of a Villiers for the sake of his own preferment and the hope of high office which had never materialized, and he envied the man who had shot Buckingham and wished he had had the temerity to have done it himself. How strange, he mused, that it was only when they were in dire straits in poverty and in the midst of an ugly war that they had found wonderful peace and happiness together.

He was glad to be going to the Marches, which was in the main solid for the King. Chester, Ludlow, Bridgnorth and Shrewsbury were all strongly fortified towns and if well provisioned could hold out for many months. Queen Henrietta had already left the country to seek aid from her brother and bring foreign reinforcements which might turn the tide and ensure victory after all, so it was essential that every single stronghold be held. His assignment was an important one and there was no possibility that he could leave his post for the foreseeable future.

He was appointed to command Bridgnorth Castle. There had been friction between two local men, both of whom wanted precedence – hence his appointment to still the discontent between them. As he approached the great hill on which the castle stood, its strong walls towering over the River Severn below, his spirits rose a little. He viewed it with a soldier's eye and recognized that the river could bring supplies and reinforcements up to Shrewsbury or down to Worcester, Gloucester and Bristol. Men, food and ammunition could travel more easily by river than by any of the muddy tracks that passed for roads. There was much to do to ensure its safety, but it was a good garrison, well placed with the ground to the east falling steeply to the river running below and sloping away more gradually to the west, but with substantial walls around it. As in Oxford, the townsfolk were inclined towards the Puritans, but as the castle stood on a tongue of land, it could, if necessary, be held on its own.

The garrison had comfortable living quarters, and as

commander his house was handsome, but there came no good news of the war and Puritan armies were reported to be drawing nearer. Within a few weeks of his arrival, he was ordered to inspect the castle of Stokesay to see whether men or ammunition were needed, and as he skirted the beautiful Clee Hill, he decided to ride a few extra miles and visit to his own estates in Clun, to see whether they had heard that his land was now in the possession of the Puritans and whether there were any changes. When he knocked at the door of Tom's house, he received a great welcome and an assurance that they had no news so far and that as far as they were concerned, the estates were still his. When Tom enquired about Lady Purbeck, Robert confided that she was still in Oxford where the conditions were bad and getting worse. 'If only,' he said, 'she was still safe with Huw and Gwyneth at the Hall of the Forest.' Tom was silent a moment and then asked whether she could not be brought there. 'I would see to her safety as I did before.' To this Robert replied, 'I could not desert my post with the war so bitter – and Bridgnorth in my charge.' Tom shuffled his feet and said softly, 'Sir, if you would trust me, I would fetch her.' 'No, no, Tom, it is altogether too dangerous. You did me and her a great service last time, but now there are soldiers everywhere ready to kill.'

Tom pronounced himself willing and eager to go and reluctantly Robert agreed that Tom should return with him to Bridgnorth to discuss possibilities, suggesting that he should in any case wait until a convoy of some sort was travelling or until he might safely accompany some cleric in the garb of a clerk. It was some weeks before such an occasion arose, but when Robert sent for him, Tom could not be found. Robert found this vexing for these opportunities were infrequent. Finally he discovered that the day after arriving in Bridgnorth, Tom had slipped away on his own. He had told friends that he felt safer alone and unescorted, pointing out that a single horseman could skirt enemy-held towns and avoid troops of soldiers far more safely than any group.

Meanwhile Robert's troubles in Bridgnorth were multiplying daily and he had scarcely time to think about anything other than the defence of the town. There was a skirmish with a band of Puritans and as they pressed their attack into the town, one of his officers, Colonel Billingsley, was killed in the local churchyard. This was a grievous loss, for he was a local man, a good leader, and well liked by the townspeople. Worse still, in their retreat towards the castle, royalist troops set fire to many houses to hamper the enemy and this caused such bitter resentment that Robert realized that he could no longer count on local people for help.

Although relatively safe within the castle, with the gates shut and the place well stocked, enemy forces now began to surround the town and he had not sufficient troops to make a sortie to repel them. They took up permanent quarters on a hillock not far away and from there began to fire cannonballs into the castle grounds. By night they came right up to the foot of the cliff and shouted a demand for surrender, and to add to his distress, scouts reported that a small posse had established themselves in a cave right beneath the castle where they were safe from overhead attack. Even if he had wished to fetch Frances himself, now there would have been no possibility, for Bridgnorth was wholly encompassed by Puritan forces.

Oxford, the Final Resting Place

L ady Hatton was still living in London, and having declared herself for Parliament, she was left unmolested. Food was scarce, although not impossibly so, and some supplies came to her from Stoke Poges. She was sixty and although still healthy and active, she was restless and unhappy. The only two people she really cared about – Frances and her grandson Robert – were both far away in hostile enemy camps and she feared that they were in growing danger as the war veered against the King. Her heart ached for them, but she felt powerless to help either. Robert was an officer in the Royalist Army and Frances had joined the King's court in Oxford and she could get no news of them.

In May a preacher from Oxford called to see her and he brought disturbing news. So long as they were not Catholic, it was not too difficult for priests to move about the country and it was mainly through them that families on opposing sides or living in enemy zones were able to communicate at all. He had learnt that Frances was ill. He did not know the nature of her sickness or how grave it was, but when conversing with other ladies in Oxford, they told him that she had not been amongst them for some days and it was reported that she was sick. Oxford, he continued, was indeed a sad city with little food or fuel and much sickness.

Lady Hatton questioned him closely, but she could get no further information, and after his departure she grew increasingly worried about her beloved wayward daughter. She could not rest, sleep would not come, and finally she decided that at whatever cost or danger or difficulty, she would go to Oxford and bring Frances to London and nurse her back to health. She was burdened by grief and remorse, for the marriage, for the angry words that had passed between them before Frances had left for Oxford, and for all the unhappiness that she had endured throughout her married life. She blamed herself for ever having given in to her husband, and yet, she mused, what would have been her fate if she had not consented. Perhaps this might be a chance to put everything to rights and gain understanding and forgiveness.

Not every nobleman had sided with the King and she decided to approach Lord Essex and demand, then ask, and finally beg for a pass to allow her to approach Oxford in reasonable safety. He was unwilling to even consider it and stressed the difficulty, the danger and the inconvenience that she would cause to everybody engaged in a brutal war. He even suggested that she was too old anyway for such an excursion, but this she ridiculed. She became so importunate and persistent, constantly reminding him of her great loyalty to Parliament, explaining again and again that Parliament owed her some consideration when she had had the courage to support it, that he finally gave her a military pass to travel as far as Thame. Beyond there, he assured her, although Oxford was virtually surrounded by Puritan forces, there was still fighting. She would get no further and he could help no more and he assured her that her journey would be entirely in vain.

Some ten days later a coach rolled up to Parliamentary Headquarters in Thame and the astonished commander was accosted by an elderly lady brandishing Lord Essex's pass and demanding help to get into Oxford. It would be utterly impossible, he spluttered in embarrassment, Oxford was still in the hands of their enemies, but she persevered, telling him that she would not, could not, return to London without her sick daughter. This worried him even more and he assured her that, even if she got into Oxford, there was no possible way to get a sick person out of the town. Still she remonstrated with him, assuring him that if he only helped to get her into the city, she would manage the rest.

She knew that spies constantly passed in and out and told him that she had heard of a spy who had reportedly seen a fight over a horse between two Cavaliers which had been settled by Prince Rupert himself with a battle axe. If such spies existed, then he could surely put her in touch with one.

The commander laughed at this and applauded her courage. Lady Hatton never stopped her persuasive talking, saying that she must help her daughter, and yes, she agreed, her daughter was on the royalist side, but she herself was a loyal Puritan, a friend of Lord Essex and anyhow, an old lady such as she was could do no harm to either side. Shamelessly, she reminded him of her close friendship with Lord Essex and assured him that she would report back on his kindness and support. At last, rather gruffly, because he was vexed with himself for giving way to her harassment, he gave her the name of someone who just might help, but she must understand the danger she was incurring and, he added, there was only a slight possibility that she would succeed.

The person he found to help her looked at her with dismay and disbelief, growling that she would get them both hanged, and she viewed him without much confidence. His face bore an ugly scar and his ragged clothing was filthy and evil smelling, but she offered him a sum that he could hardly refuse and said she would double it if they went to

Oxford that night. He looked at her doubtfully. 'How far can you walk?' he snapped and her reply came promptly, 'As far as necessary.' 'We'll leave at midnight – meet me here,' was his curt reply.

They left Thame in a baker's cart and it was a starless dark night. Lady Hatton was told to put on a long black cape and hood which covered her from head to foot and her guide put a heavy basket on her arm. 'Get into the cart, keep your mouth shut and do as I say.' She did exactly as she was bid and the pony clearly knew his way as they clip-clopped along indistinct pathways. They passed through several villages in silence, but the barking of dogs gave their presence away and once or twice she could see the light of campfires on either side, but no-one challenged them. Her guide mentioned several names as they passed, Wheatley, Garsington and finally Littlemore.

He turned the pony down a side road and into a farmyard. 'We walk from here, down the hill, over the bridge to Magdalen,' he told her, 'no more than a couple of miles.' They started off, her guide striding ahead and Lady Hatton following. Dawn was not far away now and to her relief there was a glimmer of light to guide her stumbling steps.

Suddenly, as they passed what seemed to be a ruined hovel, voices rang out. 'Stop, who goes there?' A lantern shone dimly and they were quickly surrounded by a posse of men, swords drawn. Lady Hatton's heart missed a beat, but her guide seemed unruffled. 'Tis Quinn,' he called. There was a long whispered parley and then raised voices. A soldier roughly pulled the basket from Lady Hatton's arm. 'We'll keep this for you,' and he pulled out butter, eggs and a fat hen. 'Call for 'em on your way back,' and he chuckled hoarsely at his own joke.

'Damn you all,' said the guide without any real feeling, and turning to Lady Hatton he barked, 'Don't just stand there – come along!' and they continued on their way. He was a little more affable once they had passed the guard, as if he were relieved at getting safely past them. He explained that the basket of food was the price he paid for his passage and he needed to complain loudly when it was confiscated so that, if there were strangers about, it would not be seen merely as a bribe. There were sometimes different officers who would stick to the rules and either threaten to arrest him or forbid him passage, but food was so short that anything edible commanded a good price and most soldiers were happy to accept the arrangement.

Her guide was obviously anxious to be away, and as they passed over Magdalen Bridge he took the remainder of his fee with alacrity, pointed in the direction of Merton and vanished into the misty dawn. The streets were deserted and there seemed to be no living thing awake, save for a few stray cats that slipped across her path from time to time. She walked swiftly up the High Street, keeping close to the buildings and turned right until she finally recognized Merton. She approached it and knocked at the outer porch of the college. She could see the doorkeeper asleep inside and it took many knocks before he finally stumbled to his feet and answered her call. He looked at her with hostility, his eyes still half closed and bleary with sleep, as she enquired the whereabouts of the Viscountess Purbeck. He uttered a surly oath and made as if to shut the door, but she determinedly held it open and enquired next for Lady Thynne. He admitted knowing her address, but he resolutely refused to call anyone or do business at this ungodly hour, and telling her to return later, he slammed the door shut.

It was an inauspicious start and she turned away uncertainly and stood wondering whatever to do next, when she heard the sound of horses approaching, so she slunk back into the shadows and pulled her cloak tightly round her. To her astonishment she distinctly heard the voice of Lord Suffolk. Taking courage, she stepped forward resolutely and called 'My Lord Suffolk' in a clear voice. He looked round startled at hearing his name called by a woman, uncertain where the voice was coming from, then seeing her, he dismounted and approached her. He frowned when he saw who it was and said curtly that he ought to arrest her and that she was now no friend of his and asked what was she doing here.

She spoke softly and pleaded anxiety about Frances, but his face clouded and he muttered that Frances had brought nothing but trouble to his son Robert. He demanded to know how she had got into Oxford, and when she told him, he hesitated as to what to do with her. Lady Hatton begged his assistance, pleading that they had been at court together and friends throughout their whole lives. Finally he relented and ordered one of his soldiers to escort her to Frances' lodging.

It was daylight now and she saw with disgust the dirt and squalor and smelt the evil smells of Oxford, now a closely besieged city. Mud, filth and excrement fouled every pathway, but at last they reached a small house and the soldier knocked at the door. There was no answer, so he knocked once more and after a moment of two of waiting, he put his shoulder to the door and shoved it open.

'Thank you, thank you,' she said, not wanting to enter her daughter's abode by force. 'I will find my own way now, and thank you, thank you.' Lady Hatton gave him a few coppers and sent him on his way and turned to enter a dark narrow passageway with a door opening on either side. The flagstones were bare and her footsteps seemed to sound throughout the house.

She called out several times and there was no answer, but after a while, she thought she heard a low moan. Following the sound, she pushed open the door and there lying on a low truckle bed she saw Frances, her fair hair matted with sweat and her face flushed with fever. She hurried to the bed and put her arms around her. 'Frances, Frances, this is your mother. I have come to fetch you home.'

'Oh mother, I am so thirsty.' But the words were barely intelligible.

'Is no-one looking after you?' Lady Hatton enquired, but Frances' eyes were closed and she gave no answer. Lady Hatton started looking round, first in the little room, then she went into the passage calling as she went, but the whole house was empty and deserted. At last she found a wooden beaker and filled it with water from a well outside the back door. She lifted Frances up a little and put the beaker to her mouth and she gratefully took a few sips of water before her eyes closed again and she seemed to lapse into unconsciousness.

Lady Hatton sat down beside the bed and wondered anxiously what to do, her heart sinking as it was clear that Frances was far too ill to travel in her present condition. It had been hard enough to get into Oxford alone, but to get out with a sick person scarcely able to walk would be almost impossible.

She thought of the comfort of Hatton House, the servants, the fires, the food she would give Frances and she sighed. She knew that she would have no choice but to return to

Lord Suffolk and beseech his mercy and his help. If he saw Frances as she was now, he would surely have pity on them both, and a sick woman, she would point out, was only an additional burden to a besieged city. She wondered whether he would be persuaded by her argument or whether he would simply arrest her and thus leave Frances alone and untended.

She wiped Frances' forehead with cooling water and then she looked around the house again. There were a few logs, but there was no food of any kind and no sign of anyone, so she decided that she must return to Lord Suffolk. She was just about to set out when she heard footsteps outside, then a knock on the door. Wondering whether to open it or not, she thought that it was almost certainly a messenger from Lord Suffolk and she could not afford to miss any chance of help in her present trouble, so she opened the door a little way.

A small stocky man with red hair and a ruddy beard stood there. They looked at each other for a moment. 'Madam,' he said in a gentle voice, 'T'is the Viscountess Purbeck I am seeking. Can you direct me to her lodgings?' Lady Hatton hesitated, wondering what he wanted – was he friend or foe? She had seldom been more in need of help, so she finally admitted that Frances lived here, but she was very sick. The stranger was obviously very anxious to enter and continued, 'I have a letter that I am bound to deliver to her Ladyship's own hands.' Lady Hatton countered, 'She is too sick to read a letter,' but the stranger was clearly anxious to see whether she was telling the truth and see Frances for himself and he was at least as suspicious of her as she was of him. Finally she admitted him to Frances' room and he was clearly shocked at the sight of her, lying semi-conscious, and he uttered a deep sigh.

'Who are you and what is your name?' asked Lady Hatton.

'I am Tom Feather, Madam, steward to Sir Robert Howard, Lord of Clun,' he added with pride. 'And I have orders from my master to escort my Lady to safety in Clun.'

'Tom', she said gently, 'I am her mother and I came here to take her back to London and nurse her there.' She looked down at the bed. 'I fear that neither of us can fulfil our missions at present. Shall we nurse our patient, and when she is strong and well, decide which way she should go?' Tom nodded his head in agreement.

They spent an anxious day. Lady Hatton sat by Frances' bed, cooled her hot forehead and cared for her, whilst Tom searched the town for food, firewood and medicaments. She did not dare to enquire where or how he obtained the supplies, but she was thankful and grateful for his aid.

Towards evening Frances improved a little, she drank a few drops of gruel and she recognized them both and remembered Tom's kindness to her so many years before. She even whispered of her hope for happiness. Lady Hatton put her arms around her, begging her forgiveness and Frances held her mother's hand and smiled. Then Tom pulled a letter from his pocket. 'My Lady, Sir Robert asked me to give you this.' Frances took it eagerly and pressed it to her heart before she tried to open it but her hands trembled as she fumbled with it. 'Let me help,' suggested Lady Hatton, and then they both turned away to let her read it quietly by herself. Lady Hatton removed the cup of gruel and Tom busied himself with stoking the fire.

They heard her call out, 'I am well enough to come now. Robert, my love, I am coming to you.' She threw off the bed cover with a strength they did not think she had, stumbled towards the door and fell heavily. In a moment they were both beside her and lifted her gently on to the bed. Her mother held her in her arms, her eyes were closed and she gave a little sigh before her head dropped. They tried to rouse her, but despite all their efforts, there was no pulse, no breath, no heartbeat. Frances was at peace.

Their grief was too deep for tears – indeed they had no time to mourn. It was difficult to find anybody in that beleaguered city who could organise a funeral. Finally a priest said a few hurried prayers above the coffin, whilst Lady Hatton and

Tom, an ill-assorted couple, stood silently by. Death was so common that it had lost its dignity. The coffin was lowered into the ground and earth was shovelled over it with indecent haste.

The world was indifferent to their anguish and they remained awkwardly together, uncertain where they should go or what they should do next. 'My Lady, I must help you – how will you return to London?' Tom asked quietly. Lady Hatton stood as if she could not bear to leave this grave so recently and so carelessly filled in. She gazed at the mound of brown earth, then slowly answered him. 'Tom Feather, my heart is here. I shall return to London when I please and no-one will stop me. I am safe because I no longer care what happens to me, to this country, to this war. You have a graver task. You must return to Sir Robert and tell him of our sorrow and loss, tell him why you have been unable to fulfil your task, tell him that his love, his lady, his treasure has died.'

There were tears in Tom's eyes as he said quietly, 'This is the cruellest mission that I have ever had to undertake.' Lady Hatton held out her hand to him in silent thanks. He bowed low, then took her outstretched hand, raised it to his lips, and said, 'God keep you, my Lady.' Then he turned and strode away.

About Eye Books

Eye Books is a dynamic, young publishing company that likes to break the rules. Our independence allows us to publish books which challenge the way people see things. It also means that we can offer new authors a platform from which they can shine their light and encourage others to do the same.

To date we have published 60 books that cover a number of genres including Travel, Biography, Adventure, Reference and History. Many of our books are experience driven. All of them are inspirational and life affirming.

Frigid Women, for example, tells the story of the world-record-creating first all-female expedition to the North Pole. Sue Riches, a fifty-year-old mother of three who had recently recovered from a mastectomy, and her daughter Victoria are the authors – neither had ever written a book before. Sue Riches is now a writer and highly-sought-after motivational speaker.

We also publish thematic anthologies, such as The Tales from Heaven and Hell series, for those who prefer the short story format. Here everyone has the chance to get their stories published and win prizes such as flights to any destination in the world.

And here's what makes us really different: As well as publishing books, Eye Books has set up a club for like-minded people and is in the process of developing a number of initiatives and services for its community of members. After all, the more you put into life, the more you get out of it.

Please visit www.eye-books.com for further information.

Eye Club Membership

Each month, we receive hundreds of enquiries from people who have read our books, discovered our website or entered our competitions. All these people have certain things in common: a desire to achieve, to extend the boundaries of everyday life and to learn from others' experiences.

Eye Books has, therefore, set up a club to unite these like-minded people. It is a community where members can exchange ideas, contact authors, discuss travel, both future and past, as well as receive information and offers from Eye Books.

Membership is free.

Benefits of the Eye Club

As a member of the Eye Club:

• You are offered the invaluable opportunity to contact our authors directly.

• You will receive a regular newsletter, information on new book releases and company developments as well as discounts on new and past titles.

• You can attend special member events such as book launches, author talks and signings.

• Receive discounts on a variety of travel-related products and services from Eye Books' partners.

• You can enjoy entry into Eye Books competitions including the ever popular Heaven and Hell series and our monthly book competition.

To register your membership, simply visit our website and register on our club pages: www.eye-books.com.

2006 Titles

On the Wall with Hadrian – Bob Bibby

Newly opened Hadrian's Wall path, 84 miles (135km), stretches from coast to coast and inspired travel writer Bob Bibby to don his boots and traverse the scenic and historical route. The book gives insight into Hadrian, his people and his times along with an up-to-date guide on where to visit, stay, eat and drink.

ISBN 9781903070499. £9.99.

Siberian Dreams – Andy Home

Journalist, Andy Home realises that without Norislk and its inhabitants, much of our lives in the West would need to change. So, he visits this former Prison Camp/secret city turned mining town above the Artic Circle to find out what life was really like for the 200,000 people living in sub-zero temperatures in Russia's most polluted city.

ISBN 9781903070512. £9.99.

The Good Life Gets Better– Dorian Amos

The sequel to the bestselling book about leaving the UK for a new life in the Yukon, Dorian and his growing family get gold fever, start to stake land and prospect for gold. Follow them along the learning curve about where to look for gold and how to live in this harsh climate. It shows that with good humour and resilience life can only get better.

ISBN 9781903070482. £9.99.

Changing the World. One Step at the time
Michael Meegan

Many people say they want to make a difference but don't know how. This offers examples of real people making real differences. It reminds us to see the joy and love in every moment of every day. And that making a difference is something everyone can do.

ISBN 978 1903070 444 £9.99

Prickly Pears of Palestine – Hilda Reilly
The Palestinian/Israeli conflict is one of the most widely reported
and long standing struggles in the world yet misunderstood by
many. Author Hilda Reilly spent time living and working in the
region to put some human flesh on these bare stereotypical bones
and try and make the situation comprehensible for the bewildered
news consumer.

ISBN 9781903070529. £9.99.

Also by Eye Books

Zohra's Ladder – Pamela Windo
A wondrous collection of stories of Moroccan life that offer a privileged immersion into a world of deep sensuality.
ISBN 1 903070 406. £9.99.

Great Sects – Adam Hume Kelly
Essential insights into sects for the intellectually curious – from Kabbalah to Dreamtime, Druidry to Opus Dei.
ISBN: 1903070 473. £9.99.

Blood Sweat & Charity – Nick Stanhope
The guide to charity challenges.
ISBN: 1 903070 414. £12.99.

Death – The Great Mystery of Life – Herbie Brennan
A compulsive study, its effect is strangely liberating and life enhancing.
ISBN: 1 903070 422. Price £9.99.

Riding the Outlaw Trail – Simon Casson
An equine expedition retracing the footsteps of those legendary real-life bandits, Butch Cassidy and the Sundance Kid.
ISBN: 1 903070 228. Price £9.99.

Green Oranges on Lion Mountain – Emily Joy
A VSO posting in Sierra Leone where adventure and romance were on the agenda; rebel forces and threat of civil war were not.
ISBN: 1 903070 295. Price £9.99.

Desert Governess – Phyllis Ellis
A former Benny Hill Show actress becomes a governess to the Saudi Arabian Royal Family.
ISBN: 1 903070 015. Price £9.99.

Last of the Nomads – W. J. Peasley
The story of the last of the desert nomads to live permanently in the traditional way in Western Australia.
ISBN: 1 903070 325. Price £9.99.

All Will Be Well – Michael Meegan
A book about how love and compassion when given out to others can lead to contentment.
ISBN: 1 903070 279. Price £9.99.

First Contact – Mark Anstice
A 21st-century discovery of cannibals.
Comes with (free) DVD which won the Banff Film Festival.
ISBN: 1 903070 260. Price £9.99.

Further Travellers' Tales From Heaven and Hell – Various
This is the third book in the series of real travellers tales.
ISBN: 1 903070 112. Price £9.99.

Special Offa – Bob Bibby
A walk along Offa's Dyke.
ISBN: 1 903070 287. Price £9.99.

The Good Life – Dorian Amos
A move from the UK to start a new life in the wilderness of The Yukon.
ISBN: 1 903070 309. Price £9.99.

Baghdad Business School – Heyrick Bond Gunning
The realities of a business start-up in a war zone.
ISBN: 1 903070 333. Price £9.99.

The Accidental Optimist's Guide to Life – Emily Joy
Having just returned from Sierra Leone, a busy GP with a growing
family ponders the meaning of life.
ISBN: 1 903070 430. Price £9.99.

The Con Artist Handbook – Joel Levy
Get wise as this blows the lid on the secrets of the successful con
artist and his con games.
ISBN: 1 903070 341. Price £9.99.

The Forensics Handbook – Pete Moore
The most up-to-date log of forensic techniques available.
ISBN: 1 903070 35X. Price £9.99.

My Journey With A Remarkable Tree – Ken Finn
A journey following an illegally logged tree from a spirit forest
to the furniture corner of a garden centre.
ISBN: 1 903070 384. Price £9.99.

Seeking Sanctuary – Hilda Reilly
Western Muslim converts living in Sudan.
ISBN: 1 903070 392. Price £9.99.

Lost Lands Forgotten Stories – Alexandra Pratt
The retracing of an astonishing 600 mile river journey in 1905
in 2005.
ISBN: 1 903070 368. Price £9.99.

Jasmine and Arnica – Nicola Naylor
A blind woman's journey around India.
ISBN: 1 903070 171. Price £9.99.

Touching Tibet – Niema Ash
A journey into the heart of this intriguing forbidden land.
ISBN: 1 903070 18X. Price £9.99.

Behind the Veil – Lydia Laube
A shocking account of a nurse's Arabian nightmare.
ISBN: 1 903070 198. Price £9.99.

Walking Away – Charlotte Metcalf
A well-known film maker's African journal.
ISBN: 1 903070 201. Price £9.99.

Travels in Outback Australia – Andrew Stevenson
In search of the original Australians – the Aboriginal People.
ISBN: 1 903070 147. Price £9.99.

The European Job – Jonathan Booth
10,000 miles around Europe in a 25-year-old classic car.
ISBN: 1 903070 252. Price £9.99.

Around the World with 1000 Birds – Russell Boyman
An extraordinary answer to a mid-life crisis.
ISBN: 1 903070 163. Price £9.99.

Cry from the Highest Mountain – Tess Burrows
A climb to the point furthest from the centre of the earth.
ISBN: 1 903070 120. Price £9.99.

Dancing with Sabrina – Bob Bibby
A journey along the River Severn from source to sea.
ISBN: 1 903070 244. Price £9.99.

Grey Paes and Bacon – Bob Bibby
A journey around the canals of the Black Country.
ISBN: 1 903070 066. Price £7.99.

Jungle Janes – Peter Burden
Twelve middle-aged women take on the Jungle. As seen on Channel 4.
ISBN: 1 903070 05 8. Price £7.99.

Travels with my Daughter – Niema Ash
Forget convention, follow your instincts.
ISBN: 1 903070 04 X. Price £7.99.

Riding with Ghosts – Gwen Maka
One woman's solo cycle ride from Seattle to Mexico.
ISBN: 1 903070 00 7. Price £7.99.

Riding with Ghosts: South of the Border – Gwen Maka
The second part of Gwen's epic cycle trip throughthe Americas.
ISBN: 1 903070 09 0. Price £7.99.

Triumph Round the World – Robbie Marshall
He gave up his world for the freedom of the road.
ISBN: 1 903070 08 2. Price £7.99.

Fever Trees of Borneo – Mark Eveleigh
A daring expedition through uncharted jungle.
ISBN: 0 953057 56 9. Price £7.99.

Discovery Road – Tim Garrett and Andy Brown
Their mission was to mountain bike around the world.
ISBN: 0 953057 53 4. Price £7.99.

Frigid Women – Sue and Victoria Riches
The first all-female expedition to the North Pole.
ISBN: 0 953057 52 6. Price £7.99.

Jungle Beat – Roy Follows
Fighting terrorists in Malaya.
ISBN: 0 953057 57 7. Price £7.99.

Slow Winter – Alex Hickman
A personal quest against the backdrop of the war-torn Balkans.
ISBN: 0 953057 58 5. Price £7.99.

Tea for Two – Polly Benge
She cycled around India to test her love.
ISBN: 0 953057 59 3. Price £7.99.

Traveller's Tales from Heaven and Hell – Various
A collection of short stories drawn from a nationwide competition.
ISBN: 0 953057 51 8. Price £6.99.

More Traveller's Tales from Heaven and Hell – Various
A second collection of short stories.
ISBN: 1 903070 02 3. Price £6.99.

A Trail of Visions: Route 1 – Vicki Couchman
A stunning photographic essay.
ISBN: 1 871349 338. Price £14.99.

A Trail of Visions: Route 2 – Vicki Couchman
A second stunning photographic essay.
ISBN: 0 953057 50 X. Price £16.99.